HAUNTED
GRIMSBY

HAUNTED GRIMSBY

Jason Day

The
History
Press

For my parents, Barry and Winifred Day

First published 2011

The History Press
The Mill, Brimscombe Port
Stroud, Gloucestershire, GL5 2QG
www.thehistorypress.co.uk

British Library Cataloguing in Publication Data.
A catalogue record for this book is available from the British Library.

ISBN 978 0 7524 6056 7
Typesetting and origination by The History Press
Printed in Great Britain

Contents

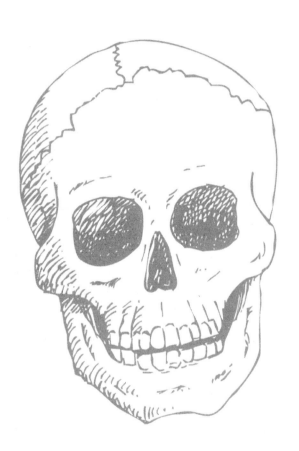

Foreword

SOMETIMES being a ghost hunter – or paranormal investigator, if you're being posh – can be an unrewarding job; it often involves sitting in the dark, being cold, getting wet and definitely getting tired, and a lot of the time you don't actually witness anything paranormal. But there are times when a cold shiver runs down your spine and you get a wild rush of adrenalin as something totally inexplicable happens, or you see something ghostly walking a lonely corridor or gliding down a grand staircase. That's when you think that what you are doing is worth it. For me, this kind of routine – and even a career – stemmed from one of my all-time passions when I was younger; reading.

I would pop to the local library and grab as many books as I could – books like the one you are reading at this very moment – about haunted houses, ghostly phenomenon and mysteries of the universe. I would sit for hours at a time mesmerised by their content.

Jason Day's *Haunted Grimsby* is as much a fascinating read as those that I have read over the years, and follows his other works – all of which are in the same vein.

While exploring locations where you might typically expect to find a ghost or two wandering around (like old coaching inns, ancient halls or even RAF airfields and bases), Jason Day has also managed to include some unique stories in his research: the haunting of the atmospheric *Ross Tiger* boat, moored at Grimsby Docks, and the Asda supercentre spectre, for example.

Whether you are a believer in ghosts or not, *Haunted Grimsby* offers a fascinating read for all – regardless of age. So choose a quiet night, make yourself comfortable in your favourite armchair, dim the lights a little and settle down to an evening with Jason Day's *Haunted Grimsby* … and I bet you it won't be long before you reach for the light switch again!

Phil Whyman, 2011

Phil Whyman is a paranormal investigator and author. He formerly worked on of Living TV's *Scream Team* and *Most Haunted* (series 2-4).

Acknowledgements

I would like to thank the following people for their help, support, patience and hard work in producing this book. Thank you to Cate Ludlow at The History Press, without whom the book would not have been possible. Also thank you to my family for their love and tireless support of my work. Further thanks go to my wife Kelly Day for her photos, to Tracie Wayling for her illustrations and to Phil Whyman for his foreword; without your brilliant contributions the book would not have been possible either. I would also like to thank paranormal investigators Andrew Killbee, Steve Dinsdale and Suzan Drury for their contributions and for sharing their findings from investigations with me and, ultimately, with you the reader. I should also thank those that have been brave enough to come forward with stories of their paranormal encounters in and around the Grimsby area, and who allowed me to share them with you. Special appreciation goes to the spirits that have managed to manifest themselves one way or another; this book will let even more people know you are out there. Finally, a big thanks to you the reader, I hope you enjoy the book.

About the Author

WRITER and broadcaster Jason Day was born and raised in Scunthorpe, where he lived for nearly thirty years until moving to Essex. Jason was the longest serving feature writer for *Paranormal Magazine*, the largest monthly paranormal publication of its kind in the UK at the time, writing over twenty articles during that period. He has also been a regular contributor to paranormal publications such as *FATE* magazine in the USA (the longest running paranormal magazine in the world) and *Ghost Voices* magazine in the UK. Jason also works with others in the written media, including some very prominent names in the paranormal community. His first book, *It's Only A Movie...Isn't It?*, was released on 1 May 2010. Jason has gone on to write *Haunted Scunthorpe* and *Paranormal Essex*.

His interest in the paranormal was sparked by his love of film and passion for reading. Jason grew up on a staple diet of 'Hammer Horror' movies and the written works of Peter Underwood, Dr Hans Holzer and Harry Price. With the advent of television shows such as *Arthur C. Clarke's Mysterious World* and *Strange But True*, Jason was hooked. He decided to begin researching and investigating cases of the paranormal for himself and the fuse was lit.

Jason's experience working in the paranormal field has been varied, ranging from his work as a co-host on the *Friday Night Paranormal Show* on Pulse Talk Radio to being the featured article

Jason Day visits Elegant Lighting, the location of one of Grimsby's most famous hauntings. (Photo courtesy of Kelly Day)

writer for the paranormal reference website ghostdatabase.co.uk. Jason is also the chief consultant for the Famously Haunted Awards organisation on MySpace. He has been a guest on numerous radio shows and has appeared at several paranormal events and given lectures about his work within the paranormal field.

Jason currently hosts *The White Noise Paranormal Radio Show* online and has interviewed such figures in the paranormal community as James Randi, Dr Ciaran O'Keeffe, Derek Acorah, Lorraine Warren, Nick Pope, Stanton Friedman, Richard Wiseman, Ian Lawman, Jason Karl and Richard Felix. Now in its fifth series and well on the way to a hundred episodes, the show can be found at the official White Noise Radio Show Website (www.whitenoiseparanormalradio.co.uk). Jason and the show won two awards at the International Paranormal Acknowledgment Awards in 2009. Jason was named 'Best International Paranormal Radio Show Host' and *The White Noise Paranormal Radio Show* was voted 'Best International Paranormal Radio Program'.

In early 2010, Jason became managing director of Phantom Encounters Ltd, an events company offering a variety of paranormal experiences to the public, ranging from ghost hunts to UFO sky watches and monster hunts. The company also hosts a paranormal lecture series and corporate events. You can find out more about Phantom Encounters events at www.phantomencounters.co.uk.

One of three founding members of a small, not for profit, paranormal investigation team based in Essex by the name of SPIRIT (Society for Paranormal Investigation, Research, Information and Truth) – established in March 2006 – Jason's commitment to researching, investigating and attempting to explain the paranormal continues. You can find out more about Jason at his official website (www.jasonday.co.uk).

Jason Day in the haunted radio room at the Fishing Heritage Centre in Grimsby. (Photo courtesy of Kelly Day)

A Brief History of Grimsby

GRIMSBY (or archaically Great Grimsby) is a seaport on the Humber Estuary in north Lincolnshire. The town itself has a population of approximately 92,000 at present. It is physically linked to the adjoining town of Cleethorpes, and 11,000 of its inhabitants live in the village of Scartho, which was absorbed into Grimsby before laws on the greenbelt were put in place.

Although there is some evidence of a small town of Roman workers sited in the area seven centuries earlier, Grimsby was founded by the Danes in the ninth century AD. According to legend, the name Grimsby originated from 'Grim's by', or 'Grim's village'. This is based on Grim the Danish Viking, supposedly the founder of the town, with the suffix – by – being the Old Norse word for village. Located on the Haven, which flowed into the Humber, Grimsby would have provided an ideal location for ships to shelter from approaching storms. It was also well situated for the rich fishing grounds in the North Sea.

Grimsby is listed in the Domesday Book as having a population of around 200, a priest, a mill and a ferry (prob-ably to take people across the Humber to Hull). By the Middle Ages, Grimsby was a town with a population of perhaps 1,500-2,000 inhabitants. During the twelfth century, Grimsby developed into a fishing and trading port and at one point ranked twelfth in importance to the Crown in terms of tax revenue. Another development during this time was the founding of an Augustinian abbey at

The Great Grimsby Coat of Arms; it is believed to date back to the middle of the seventeenth century.

Grimsby in 1132. In 1184, a nunnery dedicated to St Leonard was also founded. The town was granted its charter by King John in 1201 (a charter was a document granting the townspeople certain rights). From then on Grimsby had its own court and its own local government, and by 1218 its own mayor. During this period Grimsby did not (and still does not) have town walls. It was too small and was protected by the marshy land surrounding it. However, the town did have a ditch.

In the fifteenth century, the Haven began to silt up, preventing ships in the Humber from docking. As a result, Grimsby entered a long period of decline which lasted until the late eighteenth century.

During the sixteenth and seventeenth centuries, Grimsby was in steady decline and the population fell accordingly. In 1538, Henry VIII closed the two friaries in Grimsby. The nunnery and priory followed in 1539. Grimsby dwindled to being little more than a large village with a market, and like all towns in those days, Grimsby suffered from outbreaks of the plague; there was a severe outbreak in 1590/91.

In the late eighteenth century Grimsby revived a little. In 1768, a turnpike road was built to Wold Newton, and a new Town Hall was built in 1780. Then in 1796, an act of parliament formed a body of men who set about building new quays and deepening the Haven. By 1800 some streets were paved and even lit by oil lamps. Despite this brief upturn, the population of Grimsby, in 1801, numbered only 1,524, around the same size that it had been in the Middle Ages.

The town's fortune and population were, however, about to grow rapidly. By 1831, the population of Grimsby was just over 4,000. By 1851 it had reached 8,860

A Grimsby fisherman. (Photo courtesy of Kelly Day)

and by the end of the nineteenth century the population had ballooned to 75,000.

Grimsby boomed as a port. Iron, timber, wheat, hemp and flax were imported. In the later nineteenth century, coal, brought from the South Yorkshire coal field by rail, was exported. Many emigrants passed through Grimsby on their way to America. By 1801, the Haven was deepened. However, in the second half of the nineteenth century it was reclaimed and new docks were built. Royal Dock and the Dock Tower were built in 1852. Alexandra Dock and Union Dock were built in 1879. Number 1 Fish Dock was built in 1856 and No.2 Fish Dock followed in 1877. During the nineteenth century Grimsby's fishing fleet expanded greatly and amenities also improved in the town. In 1837, the first police force in Grimsby was formed.

The view across Alexandra Dock looking towards Corporation Bridge. (Photo courtesy of Kelly Day)

View of Grimsby from Freshney Place Shopping Centre. (Photo by Jason Day)

By 1838 gas lamps lit the streets. The arrival of the railway in 1848 made it far easier to transport goods to and from the port. In 1854, a water company was formed to provide piped water (to those who could afford it) and sewers were dug under Grimsby. A new Town Hall was built in 1863. The town gained its first newspaper in 1871 and Grimsby and District Hospital was built in 1877. Things were definitely on the rise for the town.

In 1901, the population of Grimsby had grown to 75,000. In the same year, Grimsby gained electric street lights and horse-drawn trams were replaced with electric ones. The Fishermen's Chapel was built in 1904 and Corporation Bridge was opened in 1928. By 1931, the population of the town had grown to 92,000, but then remained fairly static for the rest of the twentieth century.

During the Second World War, Grimsby's status as a major port made it a focus of the German Luftwaffe. They used the Dock Tower as a landmark and refused to bomb it (the British government discussed its demolition to prevent its use as a navigational aid). It was later thought that had the German invasion been successful, then Grimsby would have been one of the first landing points in the North of England due to the combination of its location and its infrastructure. This was probably one reason why the town suffered significantly less bombing raids than the neighbouring fishing port of Hull, whose geographical location would have made it harder to reach. However, Grimsby was still hit by numerous air raids during the war and 197 people were killed. Grimsby was also the first place in Britain to have the Butterfly Bomb used against it by the Luftwaffe in 1943, devastating many areas. The Royal Dock was used as the UK's largest base for minesweepers, to patrol the North Sea.

During the twentieth century industries in Grimsby included fishing and food processing. Despite the sharp decline in the fishing industry, since its heyday in the early 1900s, new industries came to Grimsby in the late twentieth century, such as light engineering, chemicals and plastics production.

Since the turn of the new millennium, the town has undergone a radical transformation. This long-term vision for Grimsby involves making a town which is attractive and an economically and socially desirable place to live, visit, work and play. The aim is to bring new life to the town centre by creating quality surroundings and rejuvenating the historic waterside and docks for the enjoyment of all.

With the many ups and downs encountered during its history it may come as no surprise that the town's 'haunted history' is also one filled with drama, comedy, joy and pain. Grimsby has been, and still is, a very paranormally active place, and you are about to embark on a journey through its spook-filled streets

Jason Day, 2011

Haunted Grimsby

The Supercentre Spectre

There has been much disagreement amongst the populace of Grimsby as to whether the Asda supercentre in the town is haunted or not. Some would say that there is plenty of evidence that the building has indeed been the scene of several unexplained incidents, and others maintain that these stories are just urban legend.

There have been reports of activity from staff working within the building, both in the offices and within the store and warehouse areas. On several occasions, security alarms have been triggered within the store without cause, and which, when checked, were found not to be faulty,.

Asda Supercentre is said to have experienced poltergeist activity. (Photo courtesy of Kelly Day)

The offices are reputed to be the most haunted rooms in the supercentre, with reports of office equipment such as photocopiers being turned on and off by themselves and paper being thrown to the floor by an unseen force. Some witnesses have also reported seeing a strange looking figure, which was believed to have been captured on the stores CCTV. When the footage was reviewed, the outline of a man walking back and forth in the office area was distimguishable.

In other areas of the building taps are alleged to switch themselves on and off and unexplained noises are heard. The spectral figure of the ghostly man was also seen by a cleaner at the store, who was suddenly struck by the feeling that somebody was standing beside her whilst she was working. She looked around and was greeted by the sight of a shadowy figure that appeared to be helping her by sweeping up.

Concrete evidence of this haunting is hard to come by and a lot of the evidence is 'a friend of a friend told me' or hearsay. In many cases of paranormal activity, all a researcher may have is the word of a witness or somebody that knows a witness. Perhaps the only way to find out whether this location is actually haunted or not is to take a trip down the aisles and decide for yourself.

The Black Lady and the Red Eyes

Reported sightings of the ghostly Black Lady of Bradley Woods date back to the 1920s, and other paranormal activity has also been reported in the area since the 1960s.

The woods are located along Bradley Road, just past the A46 roundabout on the B1444. The apparition of the Black Lady has been seen gliding by the entrance to the woods and in the surrounding area for nearly 100 years. She is said to be around 5ft 6in tall and wearing a black, flowing, hooded cape. Eyewitnesses describe her as young and pretty with a pale complexion and tear sodden cheeks. Encounters with her have apparently left many a witness very shaken; strangely though they are also often left with a feeling of sorrow and pity.

One evening in the 1960s, two men were travelling home from a party. As they approached the woods on Bradley Road the temperature in the car dropped dramatically. As they passed the woods and neared a bend in the road on the left, one of the men saw what he described as a white triangular blur in the field. The anomaly approached the road and as it did so, the witness saw that it appeared to be a woman in a black dress, who was now running towards the car. The driver slammed on the brakes but it was too late and the woman collided with the vehicle, making a loud thudding noise. The panicking men jumped out of the car to assist the woman, but they could see no one and the car was undamaged. They went around to the rear of the car and again there was nobody there. They checked the surrounding area and even underneath the car but they could not find anything. The men then quickly headed towards Waltham and upon arriving home they discussed what had happened that night. The only conclusion they could reach was that something paranormal had occurred and that reporting it would be pointless as nobody would believe them and they would only be ridiculed. Later, when they decided to come forward with their story, they discovered there had been several other similar experiences along the road during the same time period.

Had these witnesses encountered the notorious ghost known as the Black Lady of Bradley Woods and if so, who was she?

There are various theories as to who this spirit is and why she haunts the woods. According to one story, the Black Lady is the spirit of a nun who was based at a convent a mile and a half away at Nunsthorpe. Another rumour is that she is the ghost of a pregnant woman who was beaten to death by the father of her unborn child during the First World War. There is also a story that claims the Black Lady was a spinster living in isolation, in a cottage in the woods, who may even have been a witch. There is little, if any, proof to validate that any of these stories reveal the correct identity of the Black Lady. The most common belief, although again there is no hard evidence, is that the Black Lady lived in the woods between 1455 and 1485 (the Wars of the Roses). She lived in a cottage in Bradley Woods along with her young son and woodsman husband. Her husband set off to fight in the war, leaving his wife to bring up the child alone. Every day the woman would take her baby in her arms and carry him to the edge of the woods to await her husband's return, and every day they would return without him. Months passed with no sign of the woodsman but still his wife would continue her vigil. As the war raged on, the enemy crossed the River Humber, marching towards Lincoln and the woman set off from her cottage with her child for what would be the last time. As she left her home, she was attacked by three soldiers who ravished her and took her baby boy. They left her

The Black Lady of Bradley Woods. (Illustration by Jason Day)

on the ground humiliated, and broken, as they rode off into the woods. She spent the rest of her life wandering the woods in search of her husband and her son, until she died of a broken heart. Some people believe that this poor woman is indeed the Black Lady who, even after her death, is still searching for her husband and son in Bradley Woods.

A modern twist to this legend is that if you venture into the woods on Christmas Eve and shout, 'Black Lady, Black Lady, I've stolen your baby!' three times, the Black Lady will appear to you to take back her son.

Regardless of her identity, it is a fact that many eyewitnesses attest to having seen the ghost of the Black Lady in and around the area of Bradley Woods and Bradley Road. There are also reports that something or someone else far more terrifying may be haunting the area too.

During the 1960s, young couples would use Bradley Woods as a meeting place. One evening a young man and his girlfriend drove into the woods and parked their car. They were enjoying each other's company when suddenly the man let out a terrified scream and immediately started the car, speeding away as fast as he could. As he drove home at full speed, his petrified girlfriend asked him what he had seen. All the man could say was, 'The eyes, the eyes.' Once he was home and had had time to regain his composure, the young man was able to detail a more coherent account of his experience. The man claimed that whilst they were sitting in the car, he noticed a pair of glowing red human eyes staring at them from the darkness of the woods. He was overcome with a feeling of total terror and felt that he had to get out of the woods straight away.

This account does not tie in with the experiences of the witnesses who have encountered the Black Lady, which must lead us to consider whether there is something else, with perhaps a more evil intent, lurking in Bradley Woods?

The Ghostly Whisperer

Some cases of alleged paranormal phenomena will always be left open to speculation, purely because the evidence, witnesses and even locations no longer exist. These are the cases where all we have left is second or third hand evidence, in the form of stories passed down through the ages. The following account is a prime example of this type of case.

In the 1700s, a small cottage stood in the town of Grimsby, known as Choof Cottage. The building was well known by the townsfolk and was said to have been home to a particularly malevolent spirit. The presence was said to be so evil that it was blamed for an accident at the cottage which had resulted in several deaths.

The local people would avoid having to walk past the building as it was said that the ungodly spirit residing within its walls would whisper from the chimney to passers by, encouraging them to kill their loved ones.

Eventually, Choof Cottage was demolished and it is believed that the fiendish spirit disappeared with it.

Shadows in the Lights

One of Grimsby's most infamous hauntings began in the early part of the twenty-first century in a building on Cleethorpes Road. Between October

Locals were so afraid of the entity that haunted Choof Cottage that they would avoid walking past the building. (Illustration by Jason Day)

and November 2004, Fiona Glover moved her business, Beagles Lighting, into No.174-176 and set up shop. Almost immediately strange things began occurring in the store. Ms Glover and her colleague, Sandra Keogh, would arrive at work in a morning only to find that boxes in the storeroom had been strewn about the building overnight. They would also find that bulbs would be unscrewed from the lamps and light fixtures in the shop, with no apparent cause. During the day the front door to the shop would open, triggering an alarm. When they turned to see who was entering the premises, there would be nobody there.

Paranormal activity at Beagles Lighting increased when Ms Glover changed the layout of the store in May 2005. The following day, two light fittings came away from the wall without any logical explanation. On the same day, the shops till, which had never had any problems before,

jammed and Ms Glover's mobile phone also began experiencing interference. She believed that the changes made to the store, and therefore the building itself, had somehow upset the spirits that resided within it. Shortly after these incidents, a customer reported seeing a collection of candle shades being thrown across the shop floor by an invisible force. It was at this point that Ms Glover decided to enlist the help of paranormal investigators.

Investigators from the Lincolnshire and East Riding Paranormal Investigation Team were one of the first to investigate the building. The team carried out extensive research and investigation, including a vigil at Beagles. Co-founder of the team Steve Page came to the following conclusion: 'There is no doubt there are large amounts of activity that could possibly be classed as paranormal and unexplained.'

The activity included lights moving on their own, doors opening and closing by themselves, light fixtures dropping from the ceiling, things being thrown and footsteps echoing throughout the store. The increased amount of paranormal phenomena in the building was now being witnessed by both staff and customers at the shop. Reports escalated; one member of staff was locked in the storeroom by an unseen presence and another saw the apparition of an old man walking up the stairs to the first floor.

In an attempt to find the identity of the spirits that were haunting Beagles, Ms Glover sought the help of those that may be able to provide the answers. Mediums and a shamanic path-walker visited the store and told her that the spirits of two men and an elderly lady haunted the building. The men were called John and Tom and one of them was believed to be aggressive in nature.

As word of the haunting spread, the story gained media coverage from local newspapers and television stations. In June 2005, paranormal investigator from Living TV's *Most Haunted*, Phil Whyman, arrived at Beagles Lighting to carry out his own investigation. Just hours before Phil arrived at the location, a light bulb had mysteriously leapt out of a lamp and smashed on the floor, so hopes were high that Phil and his team would capture some solid evidence of a haunting. Phil carried out base-line experiments to use as a reference guide during the investigation and later the vigils began. Unfortunately, no significant paranormal activity was witnessed or captured during the night but Phil remained optimistic and philosophical following the investigation. 'I guess until the scientific community gives the world conclusive proof for the existence – or non-existence – of ghosts, then myself and others

in the paranormal field will do our best to make things a little clearer,' he commented.

Activity continued and eventually Ms Glover moved premises to another building on Cleethorpes Road. Beagles Lighting may have moved from No. 174-176 but it seems that the spirits that dwell in the structure had not. Elegant Lighting took over the building and it was not long before the members of staff were experiencing similar paranormal phenomena to that which had been reported by witnesses during the Beagles Lighting haunting.

The manager of Elegant Lighting, Carmen Herd, was experiencing a feeling of unease during her working hours in the shop. She also felt that she had been touched on a couple of occasions by an unseen force in the store. Carmen and other members of staff, had also been witness to objects moving around the shop and chandeliers that were fixed to the ceiling swaying of their own accord.

In early 2010, a local medium, Suzan Drury, contacted Carmen at the store. Suzan had been intrigued by the stores haunted history and wondered if she could find out any more information about the spirits that resided there by holding an overnight vigil herself. Carmen Herd agreed to let Suzan investigate, and in March 2010, Suzan, and the GRUB paranormal investigation team from Brigg arrived in the building to carry out their examination.

The team, headed by paranormal investigator Andrew Kilbee, consisted of four investigators and a medium (Suzan Drury). They began their investigation at 11 p.m., splitting into smaller groups and conducting experiments in different areas of the shop. Suzan Drury headed upstairs

The staircase where the ghost of an old man was seen by a member of staff. (Photo courtesy of Kelly Day)

Elegant Lighting, Cleethorpes Road. (Photo courtesy of Kelly Day)

to a first-floor storeroom with another investigator. They sat quietly in the darkened room and almost immediately loud bangs began reverberating around the walls. As they looked around, the two team members also noticed that some storage racks were moving in the room and anomalous blue lights were flickering. Suzan began trying to communicate with whoever, or whatever, was causing these anomalies by using her mediumistic abilities. According to Suzan there was a spirit in the room called Elizabeth, who she described as prim and proper, busy, dedicated to her work and always on the go. Elizabeth had been in her late twenties when she passed over into the spirit world. Suzan added that the storeroom had been Elizabeth's office or her home and that it was her domain. She also said

that Elizabeth was antagonised by anybody else being in the room, which may have caused her to become hostile.

Undaunted by this information, GRUB team leader Andrew Kilbee and another team member decided to hold a further vigil in the storeroom later that evening. During their attempt to make contact with Elizabeth, or any other spirits that may have been present, the investigators filmed the proceedings and attempted to capture any audio phenomena with a digital voice recorder.

Suzan Drury's group headed downstairs to the staff canteen, where Suzan believes she encountered two phantom children. She described them as being twelve and fourteen years of age and quite playful. They were not sister and brother but they were related somehow.

Light fixtures are said to move of their own accord and have even crashed to the floor in this area of the shop. (Photo courtesy of Kelly Day)

Up to seven spirits are said to haunt this location. (Photo courtesy of Kelly Day)

As Suzan called out questions to the children; an EMF meter that was being used to monitor the electromagnetic field in the canteen showed a high fluctuation, as if the levels were increasing in answer to her questions. Suzan also claims she contacted two more spirits at the shop during the investigation. These entities were the spirit of a man called George, who was an alcoholic and aged in his mid-thirties, and also a woman called Ruth, who wore a head scarf and was dressed in clothing dating from the 1940s.

The team carried out several other experiments at the location and after six hours of investigation, they headed back to their headquarters to analyse their data. Upon playing back the video footage from the vigil Andrew and his team mate had conducted in the storeroom, they saw nothing of any significance. However, after playing back the audio recording from the same vigil, they found something rather interesting and slightly disturbing. During the recording Andrew asked the spirit to come forward and give the investigators a sign that there was something there with them. At this point neither team member in the room heard a response, but on the recording there appeared to be the sound of a female voice saying 'please go away'. Was this the same spirit that Suzan Drury had claimed to have made contact with earlier in the evening?

Video footage recorded during the investigation also appears to have caught a light anomaly that, depending on the viewer's interpretation, could also be of paranormal origin. Following the 2010 investigation, medium Suzan Drury said, 'This is a mysterious place and I know the spirits are there.'

Carmen Herd, the manager of Elegant Lighting during the team's investigation, added, 'I definitely think there is something here.'

The three separate paranormal investigations that have taken place at No.174 – 176 Cleethorpes Road over a five year period, suggest that there could be up to seven different spirits haunting the building. A building that, if these figures are correct, certainly deserves the moniker which some have bestowed upon it, namely that of the most haunted building in Grimsby.

The Wandering Matron and the Loving Father

The original buildings on Scartho Road began life as a workhouse and infirmary in 1894. They were opened on 9 October by the Right Honourable J. Shaw-Lefevre, with the 10 acre site serving the ever-expanding population of Scartho. Following a local government Act in 1929, the workhouse came under the control of Grimsby Town Council and was renamed Scartho Road institute. Following the National Health Act nineteen years later, the institute became the Grimsby District General Hospital.

The hospital served the local populace for several years, and in 1974 construction began of a larger facility next to the old site. Work finished in 1982, and in the following year Princess Diana officially opened the new Grimsby District General Hospital. Following the completion of the new hospital, some of the old workhouse buildings were used for administrative or ancillary services, with the rest being demolished or simply left standing empty and unused.

After Princess Diana's tragic death in 1997, the hospital was renamed the Diana,

Princess of Wales Hospital, in her honour. The Princess' portrait hangs in the main entrance hall of the building. Visitors began to place flowers beneath the painting in memory of Diana, and the entrance hall and portrait became something of a shrine. Staff at the hospital began to notice that the flowers would seem to last rather longer than would be expected before dying and, even more curiously, the portrait of the Princess would shift position on the wall with no apparent cause.

Members of staff at the hospital have also reported seeing an apparition in one of the former workhouse buildings on the site, on several different occasions. Witnesses claim to have seen the figure of a nurse, dressed in what they describe as old-fashioned clothes. Interestingly, the ghostly nurse seems to only be visible from the knees upward. A similar manifestation has been reported by nurses, patients and domestic staff in other parts of the hospital. The description given in these accounts is that of a tall lady wearing a high, white starched hat and a long black dress. She is said to be 'matron-like', and unlike the sightings in the old workhouse, this apparition can be seen from the knees down as witnesses describe her as wearing 'squeaky shoes'. The sightings in the main hospital and the former workhouse buildings are believed to be of the same ghost, a former matron who worked at the old infirmary in the late 1800s.

Another more personal account of the paranormal involved a patient and occurred at the hospital in 2008. A female patient awoke following a surgery to find her father stroking her hair; she fell back into a state of sleep and awoke later. She recalled her father's presence and as he had passed away some time before, she assumed she had imagined the event. During breakfast the following day, the patient recounted her 'dream' and a fellow patient from the opposite bed interjected, saying that she had seen a kindly looking gentleman sitting beside the lady's bed, stroking her hair, when they had brought her back from the theatre. When she asked the man what he was doing he turned to her and smiled and said, 'Don't worry, this is my daughter.' The man then seemed to vanish into thin air. The patient who had seen the lady's father also thought she had been dreaming at the time, and it was only when they shared their experiences that both realised that they may have seen something far more real.

School Spirits

The derelict, grade II listed building that stood on Eleanor Street in 2010 had a far more grand history than its sorry-looking state suggested. The three-storey building, built in 1893, was formerly a school and then went on to become a college of art.

The building is also said to have a very haunted history and to be home to at least two unfortunate lost souls. A tragic accident apparently occurred at the school when a child drowned in the pool. The apparition of this poor child was reportedly seen in the building whilst it was still used as an educational facility.

A rather more daunting phantom, believed to haunt the building is that of a former school master. The teacher worked at the school and, unfortunately, passed away in the building on the top floor. The ghost of the school master is said to be heard walking the hallways and cracking a cane across his hand.

Part of the former school and college buildings, Eleanor Street. (Photo courtesy of Kelly Day)

Over a hundred years since its construction, the building is said to be haunted by two spirits. (Photo courtesy of Kelly Day)

The Angry Old Man

During the early 1990s, a family lived on Farebrother Street in Grimsby. The mother of the family had become inter- ested in the subject of the paranormal and began spending time with like- minded people. Her husband had little interest in the subject, so when his wife's 'paranormal friends' came around to visit, he would leave the house and meet up with his own friends.

The mother began experimenting with means of communicating with spir- its and would often hold séances at the family home. Her husband thought noth- ing of this, being a complete sceptic, but things would soon cause him to question his own beliefs. A few months after the

The angry spirit that was encountered in a home on Farebrother Street. (Illustration by Jason Day)

terms, to get out of his house. The man jumped up out of bed and turned the light on, checking the room for any other people. There was nobody there.

He went into the other room where his wife and son were still sleeping. Convinced that the loud, clear male voice was another adult male in the house, the man checked every room but again he found nothing.

Paranormal activity continued in the home for the following few months until, finally, the family called in a priest for help. The clergyman blessed the home, starting with the boy's bedroom, and the activity dissipated significantly. The father, of the family, went as far as to state that he could almost feel that the house was at peace once the priest had left. He no longer resides at the address, but as far as he is aware there has been no further activity in the building.

séances began the couple's seven-year-old son would not sleep in his own room. After going to bed he would later go into his parents' room during the night and wake them. He told them that an old man was in his room threatening him.

This became a regular occurrence, every night the same thing would happen; the boy's father decided he had had enough. To prove to his son that there was no old man in his bedroom, he decided to sleep in there himself.

The following evening the father slept in his son's room alone; his son slept in his parents' room with his mother. At around 2 a.m. the father was awoken by the sound of soft footsteps around his bed. As he had not opened his eyes yet, he assumed it was his son and shouted for him to go back to sleep. With that a gruff male voice told the man, in no uncertain

Ghostly Legs

The Fishing Heritage Centre at Alexandra Dock is a museum dedicated to preserving and depicting the history of Grimsby's fishing. The centre, opened in 1991, also hosts several temporary exhibitions throughout the year. Tours of the fishing trawler *Ross Tiger*, which is berthed at the centre, are also available to the public during visits to the museum.

The museum (including the *Ross Tiger*) is said to be the home of various spirits. Since 2003, members of staff have reported various incidents of paranormal phenomena in the building. These are said to have manifested as mysterious cold spots, smells and inexplicable sounds.

The strong smell of tobacco smoke is often experienced by staff and visi-

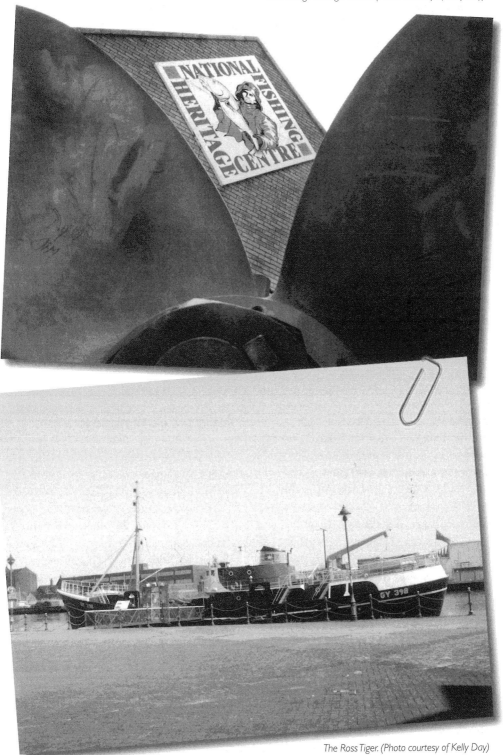

The Ross Tiger. (Photo courtesy of Kelly Day)

tors in this 'non-smoking' building; cold spots in the 'radio room' and the sounds of shuffling footsteps are heard in rooms, but there is no obvious source. A particular incident of note occurred in the gift shop of the museum. One day, a member of staff was working in the shop when they became aware of a presence in the room. The staff member had just locked up and was talking to another member of staff when she felt someone was standing behind her. She turned in the direction of the presence, fully expecting to see another colleague or member of the public standing there, but what greeted her was far more disturbing. There, standing before the witness, was a pair of disembodied legs.

Several unexplained incidents have occurred onboard the *Ross Tiger* too, with people visiting the cabins on the boat hearing footsteps on deck when nobody else could have been there and a door, which was always kept open on the trawler, being found jammed shut.

It is believed by some that the spirits present at the museum may be associated with the former timber yard that stood on the land before the museum, though others believe the ghost of a former museum tour guide (and skipper of the *Ross Tiger*), Alf Hodson, is the phantom still walking the rooms of the museum.

In 2005, an overnight paranormal investigation was carried out at the Heritage Centre, that not only focused on the museum itself but also involved an investigation of the *Ross Tiger*. The team of investigators consisted of twelve people including museum staff, researchers and experienced paranormal investigator from TV's *Most Haunted*, Phil Whyman.

The investigation began with a walk-through of the location and a number of

The haunted gift shop at the Fishing Heritage Centre. (Photo courtesy of Kelly Day)

baseline tests. This included measuring EMF levels and temperatures, and testing for natural phenomena such as creaky floorboards and drafts. The team also set up recording equipment at the location. The vigil began with the team splitting up into two separate groups, with a larger group heading for the *Ross Tiger* and a smaller group, consisting of Phil Whyman, Nick Scrimshaw and two others, staying in the Heritage Centre. This team headed for an area set up as the bridge of a trawler, complete with a skipper's table. The team sat around the table and waited to see if anything unfolded. Upon completion of their vigils, the teams swapped locations. Phil Whyman's group headed for the *Ross Tiger*, while the other team investigated various areas of the museum that were reputedly haunted, including the 'radio room' and the 'sorrow room'.

The Ross Tiger is believed to be haunted by former skipper
Alf Hodson. (Photo courtesy of Kelly Day)

The fishermen's quarters exhibit at the Fishing
Heritage Centre. (Photo courtesy of Kelly Day)

The two parties regrouped at the end of the investigation to compare and corroborate their findings.

In general, the investigation was rather uneventful and the findings were inconclusive. Some of the team were sure that there was a spiritual presence in the building and one member had an interesting experience on the stairs. As they walked up the stairs, they felt the presence of a man and stopped in their tracks. The team member exclaimed, 'He's here,' and the hairs on the back of their neck stood on end. Then, as suddenly as the feeling had come, it passed.

Although disappointed with their findings on the night, the investigators were not totally dejected. As is the nature of paranormal investigations, phenomena does not always happen on demand and there are more than enough previous

Part of a recreated street scene in the Fishing Heritage Centre. (Photo courtesy of Kelly Day)

The very eerie, and allegedly haunted, 'sorrow room' in the Fishing Heritage Centre. (Photo courtesy of Kelly Day)

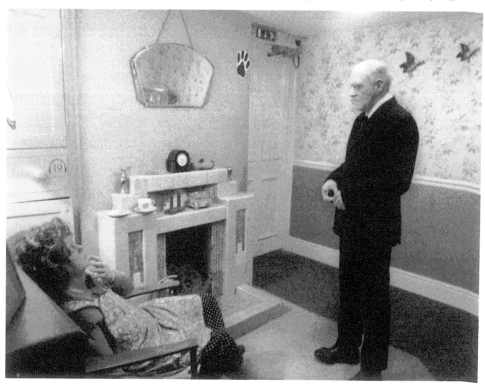

eyewitness reports from the Heritage Centre and the *Ross Tiger* to suggest that this location is indeed haunted.

The Charity Store Poltergeist

During the period that the charity Oxfam occupied the premises at No. 100 – 102 Freeman Street, they experienced an unexpected, and still unexplained, amount of paranormal activity. Witnesses included both staff and customers.

From the accounts and records that were gathered, the phenomena experienced in the building seems to have been very similar to that which is described during a poltergeist infestation. The duration of the phenomena, which seemed to

The former charity store that was plagued by poltergeist activity. (Photo courtesy of Kelly Day)

dissipate just as quickly as it had begun and occurred over a period of months rather than years, also seems consistent with poltergeist activity.

Reports first began with members of staff experiencing 'cold spots' and hearing their names being called when they were in the shop alone. Electrical appliances began acting erratically in the shop; the lights flickered and the store computer started to malfunction. When these problems were looked into by technicians, they could find no fault with either the electrical sources or the appliances themselves.

The activity quickly increased and became more physical. Goods began flying off the shelves with such force that it could not simply have been caused by vibrations, or any other logical explanation. Even if it could have been explained by natural vibrations, the staff were also reporting that the walls were vibrating to such an unusual level that they thought the shelves may actually fall from the walls completely.

The closest anybody came to seeing an apparition during the haunting was when an eyewitness observed a misty form floating at the top of the stairs. The mist appeared for a few seconds before evaporating.

Phantom Nuns

Grimsby Institute stands on the site of a former nunnery, which became the priory of St Leonard some time during the reign of Henry II. The name of the founder of the priory is unknown, but the house was placed under the protection of the Austin Canons of Wellow in 1184. The priory was a poor and obscure one; its worth was valued at only 3s in 1291. By 1296, the nuns had to beg to support themselves, and in 1297 some men were excommunicated for an 'unjust distraint' upon their property. Another licence to beg was granted in 1311, on the grounds that their houses, corn, and other commodities had been consumed by fire. Yet another licence to beg was granted in 1459 because their 'buildings had been burnt and their land inundated'. In 1394, they were excused from payment of a subsidy at the bishop's request, on account of their poverty. In spite of its scant revenue, the priory lingered on until 15 September 1539, when the last prioress, Margaret Riddesdale, received a pension of £4 and the other nuns received annuities of either 30s or 33s 4d.

Nearly 500 years later, numerous reports would suggest that the ghosts of the bygone nuns still wander the former priory grounds. The building itself may be long gone, but eyewitnesses regularly report seeing the apparitions of the phantom sisters amongst the trees and the bushes in the grounds of the Grimsby Institute. They have even been known to wander onto the pavement beyond the grounds, which looks onto the aptly named 'nun's corner' roundabout. One brief account, from the 'Haunted Lincolnshire' website, tells of two brothers who may have encountered the ghostly nuns here.

Late one evening, the men were walking by the roundabout when they saw what they described as a 'dark shadow' run across the road and straight into the path of an oncoming lorry. The driver

of the vehicle slammed his brakes on and brought the truck to a halt. He then jumped out of his cab, only to find that there was nobody there. Whatever ran out in front of his lorry had vanished. The brothers confirmed that as the vehicle had 'struck' the shadowy figure, it had indeed disappeared before their very eyes.

The Evil Spirit

During the 1950s, a section of sidings along the Grimsby to Cleethorpes railway line developed something of an eerie reputation. Many men who were asked to work in the area simply refused, or reluctantly went about their duties as hastily as possible.

The sidings were used, amongst other things, to connect vacuum pipes to wagons on special vans that carried fresh fish between Cleethorpes and Grimsby. One particular evening, a shunter was attaching pipes to a wagon when he developed an all too familiar feeling that something wasn't quite right. He hastily completed his task and rushed back to the driver. When the driver tested the pressure on the brakes, it became clear that the pipes weren't connected properly. The shunter was reluctant to address his error so a fellow shunter went back to the wagon to check the pipes. The second man could not find a problem, so the engine driver tested the pressure again. Once more it was too low. A third man went to check the pipes and, as he left the company of his colleagues, he was overcome with a feeling of dread. The feeling grew as he went about his task and when his torch began to flicker for no apparent reason, he began to feel as if something malevolent was nearby. As he finished his check, a foul stench began to fill the air and he ran back to the safety of of his work mates.

On his return, the third shunter relayed to the engine driver that he too could find no fault with the pipes. The driver was furious and gave the shunters a piece of his mind, questioning both their capabilities and workmanship. He then led the group back to the wagon for a final check. As they reached the wagon, all of the men's torches began to flicker and the foul smell returned. The shunters began to shake and sweat with fear as the driver checked the pipes and found a loose connection. The driver was also becoming affected by the atmosphere as he corrected the fault, and upon completion all four of the men ran as quickly as they could back to the engine.

Some years following this incident, a man wandered out to the haunted sidings. He stood in the spot where the feeling of evil was said to be the strongest and, in the cover of darkness, knelt down and placed his neck on the railway tracks. He was beheaded by a wagon passing over the track.

The fear-inducing, malevolent spirit, which some say may even be demonic, may still inhabit the line between Grimsby and Cleethorpes; so beware!

The Grimsby Scratcher

The Sayles family moved into a house in the north-west of Grimsby in 2007, and initially everything appeared to be going well. Lynn Sayles, her husband Dave and their two children were all enjoying life in their new home, until a bizarre series of events turned their lives upside down.

On Sunday 6 May, Lynn and Dave settled down in front of the television to watch an episode of *Most Haunted*. This was a reality television show in which a group of paranormal investigators, mediums and a presenter go to a haunted location and try to find any evidence of a haunting. There were also live episodes of the show aired occasionally and it was one such live show that the Sayles were watching that night in May 2007. The episode was broadcast live from Redcliff Caves in Bristol and featured such experiments as psychic art, automatic writing and using an Ouija board. Following the program, Lynn decided to try a psychic art experiment of her own. She picked up a pen and some paper and opened up her mind, attempting to channel the images of any spirits that were around her at the time and draw their portrait. Little did she know, they were closer than she had imagined. In an interview with the *Grimsby Evening Telegraph*, Lynn recalled, 'I got a pen and started writing … somehow my mind had opened up [to] a bad spirit that was releasing these psychic thoughts.'

Lynn was not creating psychic art, as she had intended, but was in fact producing automatic writing. She was channelling a spirit who was generating the writing through Lynn's hand. She produced page after page of writing, and when the session finally came to a close Lynn and her husband read back through the transcript and found that, in the past, a sad and horrific story had unfolded in their neighbourhood.

The automatic writing implied that the spirit of a man named Mark Ripley had come through to Lynn. Mark said that his partner, Mary, had been taken away from him, raped and killed. Mark's spirit wandered the area in the hope of being reunited with Mary. The automatic writing also suggested that Mary's spirit resided within Lynn Sayles' home and although Mark's spirit roamed the area too, for some, as yet unknown, reason they were still unable to reconnect in the spirit world.

Over the following week or two, the family began to experience mild, inexplicable occurrences; ones that are often attributed to paranormal activity, such as dramatic drops in temperature and a feeling of being watched. Lynn was particularly concerned with the activity in one of the bedrooms, which she believed Mary was haunting. Lynn and Dave decided to enlist the help of a vicar to 'reunite' the spirits of Mark and Mary, which they hoped would then bring an end to the haunting. The vicar came and blessed the house, but this only served to escalate the ghostly activity after he had left.

The couple first noticed that the lights in the house began switching themselves on and off, especially the light at the top of the stairs. This became such a regular occurrence that the light seemed to be flashing constantly, as if somebody, or something, was trying to draw their attention. Then other electrical appliances took on a life of their own. In the kitchen, the kettle started turning itself on and boiling, and the computer sparked into life without being switched on by anybody in the house. Thinking there may be a rational explanation for this, such as some kind of wiring fault, Dave turned the electricity off at the main supply. The anomalies continued and increased.

The children in the family were also becoming aware of the paranormal activity. The Sayles' son told his parents that voices were telling him to get out bed in the morning and play with his toys. He told them he had also witnessed other strange things. A football had rolled across his bedroom floor by itself and his battery-operated toys were making sounds and flashing their lights, even when they were not turned on.

Lynn and Dave were becoming increasingly disturbed by what was happening to them and it was not long before things escalated to such a degree that they sought outside help once more. Dave awoke one morning and dressed. He folded the shorts that he slept in and put them on his bed. The shorts stayed there all day and when he returned to his bedroom that evening they were still there, folded up on the bed. He undressed and picked up his folded shorts; as he lifted them and they unfolded he was met by a horrific sight. His shorts had been torn to shreds. Dave rushed out of the bedroom in fright and ran downstairs, with the shorts in his hands, to show Lynn. His wife assured him that nobody had been in the bedroom and that the shredded shorts must be attributed to the paranormal activity that was occurring in their home. As they talked, Dave felt a pain in his ankle. He looked down to discover that something or someone had scratched him. He noticed that there were three definite scratches on his ankle, resembling the marks one would receive if they were scratched by human nails or a small animal's claw. Lynn commented that, in his haste to leave the bedroom, he may have caught or knocked his ankle against something like the doorway or furniture. Dave was adamant that he had not and, in fact, was scratched again later that day by an unknown source. Over the next two days Dave received more unexplained scratches about his body; every time they were the same, always a set of three. The Sayles had had enough. It was one thing that the entity, or entities, in the house were switching things on and off, making noises and moving things, but the fact that they were now causing physical harm could not be overlooked.

This time Dave and Lynn did not seek help from the church, they sought out another spiritual source – a psychic medium. Mediums are said to be able to communicate with the spirits of those that have passed away, and some are even said to be able to cross wayward spirits into the next realm. Local medium Graham Francis was called in and immediately he was drawn to the second bedroom. This was the room that Lynn believed was haunted by the spirit of Mary. Graham felt there had been a presence in the room and experienced a distinct drop in the room's temperature whilst he was in there. As Graham descended the stairs, he sensed he had made a connection with a spirit. Graham told the couple that he had indeed interacted with a spirit in the home, but the spirit was neither that of Mark nor Mary. Upon reaching the foot of the stairs Graham had seen the ghost of an old man sitting on the bottom step smoking a pipe. The spirit seemed very angry that his peace had been disturbed and was making it quite clear to Graham that he saw the Sayles family as strangers who had invaded his space. It was very apparent to Graham that, as far as the spirit of the old man was concerned, Lynn and David were not welcome in the property.

The activity continued and escalated once more. Lynn was now being scratched by the invisible assailant and one such episode culminated in her having very noticeable scratch marks on her shoulder. Medium Graham Francis was still trying to help the family, and one afternoon Dave was upstairs whilst Lynn was downstairs with the children waiting for Graham to arrive. There was nobody else in the house at the time. Dave began making his way downstairs when he heard a vicious masculine voice call out, 'Will you hurry up!' With that there was a crashing sound of breaking glass and Dave ran down the stairs. Upon reaching the living-room door, he discovered one of the glass panels in it was smashed and glass was strewn all over the floor. He rushed into the kitchen and found Lynn bleeding heavily from a large gash in her foot.

The Grimsby Scratcher. (Illustration by Jason Day)

Lynn was taken to the local hospital and received several stitches in her injured foot. To this day, it is not known exactly what happened during the incident, but medium Graham Francis believes the spirit of the angry old man had more than a passing involvement. Graham suspected that the spirit knew he was about to visit the house that day, and by causing the accident, he hoped to deter the Sayles from continuing their interaction with a medium. Graham believed this theory was supported by the fact that Lynn's injury occurred just as he was walking through the front gate of the Sayles' garden that afternoon.

The family were now at their wits' end with the haunting and were sleeping together downstairs. They decided to turn to a rather unconventional option in their search for a solution; a paranormal television show.

Lynn and Dave contacted Original Productions. This company was looking for allegedly haunted homes to film at for episodes of their Living TV show *Living with The Dead*. Series producer Richard Greenwood said, 'It was a good story from our perspective, whereby the paranormal activity got so extreme they wanted to move out. Something had to be done, especially as they had two young kids.'

The premise of the show is that the *Living With The Dead* team, psychic medium Johnnie Fiori, medium and exorcist Ian Lawman and paranormal investigator Mark Webb (other investigators featured on the show included Andy Matthews and Stephen Griffiths), work together with home owners who are seeking help with their unwanted spiritual house guests. The first member of the team to arrive at the Sayles' home was Johnnie Fiori. Johnnie met the family

and, after hearing about how the haunting had begun, told them she believed that Lynn may have opened a vortex for spirits to come in and out of, by attempting the automatic writing in the house. Johnnie began a tour of the building and, like the medium who had visited the house before her; she too was drawn to the second bedroom. Upon entering the room, Johnnie was hit by an icy cold temperature drop. This phenomenon is believed, by some, to signal the presence of a spirit. She also felt the energy of a spirit in the corner of the bedroom, and a general aura of anger in the room overall. At the end of her visit, Johnnie gave the family spiritual protection and left.

During February 2008, Lynn and Dave had been filming the alleged paranormal activity in the house on their video camera. The footage (aired during the show) showed Lynn filming in a room where there seemed to be a noise coming from the computer. Despite her best efforts she could find no apparent source. Lynn also recounted seeing a black shadow moving across the second bedroom with a white light following it.

The next team member from the *Living With The Dead* show, medium and exorcist Ian Lawman, then arrived at the house. The children had gone to stay with friends for the evening while Ian, Lynn and Dave investigated the house together. Firstly, Ian used his mediumistic abilities to try and pick up any spirits present. Whilst on the stairs, Ian experienced a choking sensation, as if he were being strangled. He sensed an aggressive male figure on the stairs, much like medium Graham Francis had on his visit to the home. Again, like Graham, Ian sensed that the male spirit was evil and wanted to 'punish' people. Ian (like Johnnie Fiori and Graham Francis) was also drawn to the second bedroom. He felt the energy of a small child in the room, who he believed was between five and seven years old. The phantom child was afraid of the spirit of the man and often ran away from him when he was close. Whilst Ian was in the second bedroom, Lynn and Dave moved into the adjacent bedroom and began investigating. As they looked around in the dark, there was a sudden, loud, unexplained noise and Lynn ran down the stairs. Ian and Dave then followed suit.

In the living room, Lynn and Dave began a Ouija board experiment to try and communicate with the spirits whilst Ian observed. As the couple called out, the glass began to move in response. As the energy built, the table itself began to move and eventually toppled over. At this point Lynn ran from the room terrified, and actually left the house. Later she returned to the living room and joined Ian and Dave.

They then decided to hold a séance. As they joined hands around the table and began, they heard banging noises in

Medium and exorcist Ian Lawman believed there were two entities residing at the residence in the Grimsby Scratcher case; a small child and a dark man. (Illustration courtesy of Tracie Wayling)

the room. A short time into the séance, Lynn proceeded to channel a spirit that seemed to be the evil male. The spirit said his name was George and that he wanted the family out of the house. As the channelling became more intense, Ian decided that it was too dangerous for her to continue and brought Lynn forward out of her trance. In an effort to further communicate with George, Ian used his own mediumistic abilities to channel the spirit of George himself. As George's spirit came through Ian, he shouted at Dave and Lynn that it was his house. Dave then responded by telling George that it wasn't his house anymore and that he should leave. There then began a heated exchange between George (through Ian) and Dave. Finally, Ian came out of the trance and the investigation was over.

Living With The Dead team member and paranormal investigator, Mark Webb, had also visited the home during the investigation and carried out several experiments and tests. Following analysis of his research at the home, unfortunately Mark could find no solid, scientific evidence of a haunting to accompany the spiritual evidence obtained by the mediums.

Shortly after the investigation, Dave Sayles told the *Grimsby Evening Telegraph* that the filming of the show had been more difficult than he had anticipated: 'When they filmed it was very stressful. We had to do a lot of reconstructions … it made it really intense.'

Both Dave and Lynn reported that after the *Living With The Dead* team's investigation of the house, their home seemed quieter, calmer and warmer. It seemed as if the evil entity had moved on. However, Lynn still felt uneasy in the house and had bad memories of the haunting. Shortly after the filming of the

program, the Sayles family relocated to another home in the area. Following the move Dave Sayles said, 'It has all stopped now since we moved. It is such a relief.'

Living TV aired the episode of the *Living With The Dead* show that featured the Sayles' story on 17 June 2008. The episode was entitled 'The Grimsby Scratcher'. With the family having moved away from the house, some questions still remain unanswered. Does the paranormal activity continue in the house? Are the spirits of Mark, Mary, George and the small child still residing there? Which, if any, of these entities was the infamous Grimsby Scratcher? Will we ever know?

The Restless Boy

The Old Coach House is a substantial, end-of-terrace property on the corner of Bethlehem Street, Church Street and Wellowgate, on the edge of Grimsby town centre. The building is one of Grimsby's oldest pubs and consists of spacious and versatile accommodation including trading areas, the six-bedroom owner's accommodation, storerooms, various disused rooms, outbuildings and two self-contained retail units.

The pub has had several reports of a dark, shadowy figure, no more than 4ft tall, being sighted along the corridors. The figure is reputed to be an unfortunate young boy, who began haunting the building after he was tragically killed in an accident in the barn. The barn was used to look after patron's horses whilst they were partaking of the hospitality at the inn. However, there are conflicting stories as to how the child met his death in there. One story says the boy was employed to help tend the mounts and assist the blacksmith. One day the black-smith instructed the boy to hold a horse's leg whilst he replaced a bent horseshoe. The horse reared and knocked the boy to the ground and, before he could get out of the way, the horse's hoof crashed to the ground, landing on the boy's head, crushing his skull and killing him instantly.

Another tale tells of how the boy was killed following an accident involving a coach in the barn.

Whatever his fate was, the boy is said to be the main spirit haunting the building. However, some believe he is not the only ghost in the Old Coach House. Another spirit which is said to haunt the pub is the ghost of a patron who was stabbed to death in the bar. This spirit is believed to be responsible for the 'feeling of unease' encountered by many in the building, along with the unexplained cold spots.

In September 2010, the Old Coach House was sold to a local property speculator/pub operator, who reportedly intended to reopen the pub and rent out the outbuildings and self-contained units as soon as possible. It remains to be seen as to whether the shadowy figure and the ghostly young boy moved out with the previous owners.

The Lost Airmen

RAF Waltham was opened as a heavy-bomber station in November 1941. The airfield had previously been a private flying club in the 1930s and a reserve flying-training school for the Air Ministry. The new incarnation of the airfield and station was officially named Grimsby, although the name 'Waltham' persisted among locals and servicemen at the station.

During the Second World War, the station was home to No.142 and No.100 squadrons, who regularly flew bombing operations from Waltham. The enforced break-up of No.142 squadron followed, leaving only No.100 squadron remaining at the base. The No.100 squadron made Grimsby its home until 2 April 1945 when, owing to deterioration of the runways, a move was made to RAF Elsham Wolds. This marked the end of Bomber Command flying units at the station. Operations from Grimsby saw 164 bombers lost; some fell missing in action while others crashed in the UK. These consisted of forty-eight Wellingtons and 116 Lancasters.

In the immediate post-war years, the hangars were used by No.35 maintenance unit for storage and the airfield reverted to agricultural use. Eventually the hangars were also decommissioned and reverted to commercial use. In later years, improvements to the A16, with a bypass for Holton-le-Clay, reclaimed part of the eastern side of the base, and some of the other land was bought up by property developers. Parts of RAF Waltham still remain to this day; several of the former airfield's buildings still survive, as do, according to many reports, some of the base's long-deceased airmen.

One of the earliest reports of paranormal activity to come from the former RAF base, involved a property that had been built in 1967 on the old perimeter of the airfield, near to the former location of the main gates. In 1969, the Burchell family lived in a house that was built on the foundations of one of RAF Waltham's former Nissen huts on Cheapside Road. Late one evening, Susan Burchell awoke to find a figure standing in her bedroom. Although startled and shaken, Susan had the presence of mind to reach for her bedside lamp and turn it on to illuminate the darkened room. The light revealed that the figure stood at the foot of her bed was a young, red-haired man dressed in the uniform of an airman. The man also appeared to have only one arm, as one sleeve of his jacket was pinned to his shoulder.

Susan lay frozen to her bed as the spectral airman continued to stare at her. She began screaming and the figure slowly moved towards a wardrobe and disappeared into it. Her parents were awoken by Susan's cries and rushed into her bedroom. They searched the house, including the wardrobe, and found nothing. They also checked the garden but there was no sign of anybody there either. As far as the family were aware, the airman never returned during their occupancy,

but they moved out of the house shortly afterwards nevertheless.

The location of the Burchell's home is said to hold the key to the haunting and, indeed, the phantom airman that haunted it. An airman who served at the base was said to have been declared unfit to fly, following injuries he had sustained in previous missions. Severely depressed and immensely unstable after receiving this news, the airman entered a hut on the base and pulled the pin on a grenade he was holding. The blast killed him immediately and destroyed the building. This was the very site where the Burchell home was built.

In nearby Holton-le-Clay, RAF Waltham's former hangar was also reputed to be haunted. At the time, the building was being used as a storage facility for E. W. Nickerson & Co. Staff here reported

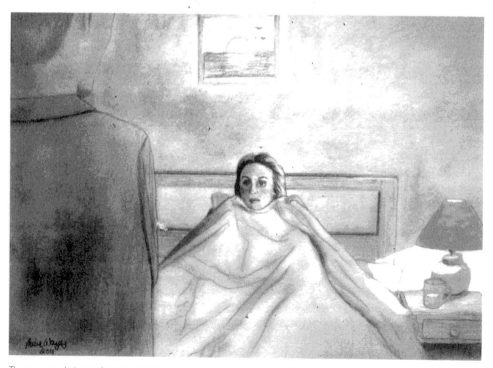

The one-armed airman that appeared in a bedroom on Cheapside Road. (Illustration courtesy of Tracie Wayling)

disturbing accounts of paranormal activity. During a night-shift one evening, an employee was repairing grain sacks in an ante-room at the end of the hangar. Late into his shift he saw something from the corner of his eye that caught his attention. As he looked up from his work, the employee saw the figure of a headless airman, in full flying gear, pass through the hangar wall into the ante-room where he sat working. Frozen into his seat with fear, the employee watched the airman as he paused for a few seconds directly in front of him and then proceeded to walk across the room and out into the hangar. The terrified employee then jumped from his seat and dashed into the hangar screaming at the top of his voice. His colleagues came to his aid and said that he was in such a state of shock that his hair was actually standing on end. When they managed to calm him down enough to relate his experience to them, they searched the hangar for any intruders, or even a workmate that may have been playing a practical joke. They found no evidence of either. It would appear that the old hangar was storing something other than machinery, grain and sacks.

These were by no means the only apparitions witnessed in the area; in fact several ghostly airmen are said to have walked along the ageing airstrips and perimeter roads at RAF Waltham over the years.

Several 'courting couples' have witnessed shadowy figures and unexplained noises. In 1982, a phantom airman was reportedly seen walking up and down a former runway before vanishing into the darkness.

One of the most recent and common phenomena reported by witnesses

The phantom airman seen disappearing into a wall at a storage facility on the former RAF Waltham site. (Illustration courtesy of Tracie Wayling)

involves a nearby road on the eastern side of the former airfield, where a memorial to the men of No. 100 squadron was erected. A spectral airman is regularly seen standing by the memorial stone at dusk; perhaps even ghosts feel the need to pay their respects to their fallen comrades.

The Phantom Fisherman

During the 1980s, No. 19 South Saint Mary's Gate was home to the Shoe Factory Shop. The manager of the shop, Mary Frost, once reported watching a white-haired old man, who wore yellow tweed trousers – like Rupert the Bear – walk across the shop floor and straight through a wall. Mary had seen a ghost, and she wasn't the only one to experience paranormal phenomena in the shop, or the flat above it.

Customers and staff alike encountered a catalogue of unexplained phenomena, ranging from unusual odours to more extreme poltergeist activity. Whole rows of shoes would mysteriously fall from their racks onto the floor, whilst doors opened and closed of their own accord in full view of staff and customers. Shoppers also recounted the feeling of having their feet tickled as they tried on shoes. There were also several instances of a strong smell of tobacco pervading the air in the store, but smoking was strictly forbidden. Other members of staff also reported seeing the apparition of an old man that matched the description of the figure seen by their manager, Mary Frost.

The haunting was not only confined to the Shoe Factory Shop itself; there was also paranormal activity experienced in the flat above the shop. A visitor to the flat described seeing a shadowy figure in the

The former Shoe Factory Shop, home of the 'phantom tickler'. (Photo courtesy of Kelly Day)

kitchen. The 'vaguely outlined' apparition floated across the room before disappearing in front of the witness' eyes. In a strange coincidence, the tenants in the flat reported experiencing the sensation of having their feet tickled, much like the customers in the shoe shop below.

The phantom, feet-tickling old man was believed to be an old fisherman who lived in one of the cottages that occupied the land where the shop now stands.

Three decades later (at the time of going to press), the building is occupied by a firm of solicitors, and it would seem that the haunting has ceased.

The phantom fisherman.
(Illustration by Jason Day)

Haunted Homes

The spirits of the deceased are said to be able to manifest themselves in environments that have been charged with the energy created by emotions. Most homes have been the scene of emotional outbursts, whether they are of great happiness or great sadness. It should come as no surprise then that many houses are said to be charged with these energies and, consequently, the residual energies provide spirits with a fuel from which they summon the ability to create paranormal activity.

One such home is located on Weelsby Road. The house is built on the site of a former nunnery and it is the ghosts of the sisters that are believed to haunt the property. The occupants of the house have heard footsteps around the building, even when there is nobody else present. Another phenomenon that has been experienced within the home is the sound of laboured breathing, which has been both heard and felt by the residents. One of the spirits responsible for the paranormal activity, which was witnessed in the house, is believed to be the Mother Superior of the former convent, who was said to have suffered from chronic asthma.

Another home that experienced similar activity to the house on Weelsby Road was a property on Langton Drive. This building was haunted by the apparition of a monk, it was witnessed by several different people, on numerous occasions. His appearances became so regular that, eventually, the family abandoned their home, never to return.

A ghostly monk was also said to have been responsible for the haunting in a council house on Newton Grove in 1967. A family claimed that the phantom monk turned on the gas taps in their house during the night, thus endangering their lives. Eyewitnesses reported that the malevolent apparition was an ugly old man dressed in a monk's habit. Unable to cope with their uninvited guest, the family, unsurprisingly, fled their home. Subsequent occupants claimed to have similar experiences and put in requests to be re-housed by the council. The paranormal activity only ceased once all of the gas appliances were removed and the house had been converted to an 'all electric' building.

The Nun and the Ghostbuster

Parapsychologist Robin Furman is the definitive authority on hauntings in the Grimsby area. With decades of research and investigation behind him, there is little he does not know about local hauntings. So, it may not come as a surprise that Robin has had at least one local phantom encounter of his own. During an interview with Trisha Nymh in *The Witchtower* magazine in 2007, Robin explained:

> The first ghost I ever saw appeared on the landing of my house in Grimsby about twenty years ago. It's a big, old house in a place known locally as Nun's Corner, because there is a theological history to the site, going back to the 11th century. I suppose, in view of that, I should not have been surprised to find a ghostly nun in the house.

During the early 1980s, Robin Furman was a businessman living in the Nun's Corner area of Grimsby. Upon going upstairs one evening, he noticed movement on the landing and thought it may be one of his children. He continued up the stairs and came face-to-face with the apparition of a nun. Robin went unexpectedly cold as he stared in shock at the unannounced guest on his landing. The nun was wearing an old-fashioned habit and veil and seemed almost tangible. As Robin looked into her veil, he noticed she had no face, but instead only a glowing light where her face should have been. She then drifted away, after what had been a very quick and startling encounter.

Following his experience, the phantom nun was also seen in the house by both Robin's daughter and son. His daughter, Victoria, was sick in bed and saw the nun sitting on the end of her bed, while his son, Andy, encountered the apparition downstairs. Andy was in the music room and, as he went to leave, he saw the nun in the doorway, blocking his exit. In his haste to escape he actually ran through the doorway and, consequently, through the nun. He described the feeling as being like he had ran through a fog.

Living in what he had discovered to be a haunted house led to Robin's interest in the paranormal. As a mature student

The ghostly monk of Langton Drive. (Illustration by Jason Day)

he took degrees in both psychology and philosophy and went on to found one of the UK's first paranormal investigation teams, Ghostbusters UK, or as they became more widely known, 'The Grimsby Ghostbusters'. Robin has gone on to become one of the leading paranormal investigators in the UK.

The Haunted Abbey

Wellow Abbey was founded by King Henry I in the early 1100s and was dedicated to St Augustine and St Olaf. The abbey was situated on a hill in the centre of Grimsby, not far from St James' Church, in the area that is now in and around Abbey Drive and Abbey Park Road. During the 1300s, the abbey was frequently in debt, mainly thanks to the abbot of the time, John Utterby. Despite the near financial ruin of the abbey during this period, the reduction in expenses by the bishop saw the abbey continue until the 1530s. In 1534, the abbot, Robert Whitgift, and ten canons signed the acknowledgement of royal supremacy and the abbey was dissolved two years later.

Parapsychologist Robin Furman saw a phantom nun at his Grimsby home in the 1980s. (Illustration by Jason Day)

By the Victorian era, the abbey was a distant memory in the town's history. A house stood on the former abbey site and paranormal phenomena was reported. The occupants of the house reported seeing apparitions of phantom monks and spectral knights in the building. The sound of a horse-drawn carriage was regularly heard coming down the driveway to the house and pulling up at the main entrance, but when the residents would open the door to welcome their visitors, there would be nobody there. Abbey House, as it became known, was eventually demolished in 1967; however, the hauntings did not stop there.

Other people also experienced paranormal phenomena on and around former abbey land. One witness owned a shop that was located very close to where Abbey House had been located.

A spectral knight allegedly haunted the old Abbey House. (Illustration by Jason Day)

Almost immediately, the owner began to notice small things that 'weren't quite right' about the building. The shop always seemed very cold, even on a hot summer's day, and the occasional unexplained noise would be heard. One day, the witness was reading a book and for some strange reason they felt there was somebody in the room with them. As they looked up, they saw the figure of a monk. Just as soon as they had seen the figure it vanished. The figure was seen by the same person several times in the building and even in the car park. Each time the phantom monk would vanish as quickly as he had appeared. Given the history of the location, it would seem quite possible that the former monks of Wellow Abbey are still serving from beyond the grave.

The Noisy Spirit

Number 31 Wellowgate is a large warehouse-like building that has, in the past, primarily been used for commercial and business purposes. As recently as 2008, the snooker club Cue World was located there before moving to premises on Victoria Street. Prior to the building being a snooker club, it was used by a local paint supplier, and it was during this occupancy that unexplained activity began occurring.

Staff working downstairs at the paint suppliers began hearing a banging noise from a room on the top floor of the building. One of them went to investigate the source of the commotion and as they entered the room the sound stopped as suddenly as it had begun. It was only then that they realised there was nobody else in the room that could have been making the noise. Following subsequent

A shopkeeper encountered a phantom monk at the premises close to Abbey House. (Illustration courtesy of Tracie Wayling)

enquires, the member of staff discovered that there had not been anybody in the room previous to, or during, the time that the banging had occurred.

The instances continued and still no explanation could be found. The noises began again one morning and a member of staff, once again, went to investigate. They opened the door to the room and the banging stopped; as they turned around to leave the room the banging started up again. The witness turned to see where the noises were emanating from, and much to their bewilderment, they saw the floorboards moving as if someone or something was stamping on them, but yet again there was nobody else in the room.

The mysterious noises continued in the building and, on a later occasion, a witness claimed to have actually seen the figure of a black monk in the haunted room. Was this apparition responsible for the noises that came from the upstairs room? Had he made the floorboards move? Who was he and why was he there? As yet these questions remain unanswered.

The Accident that Wasn't

There are many tales of phantom hitch-hikers and road ghosts throughout the country; it would seem that Britain has an abundance of such cases. This does not make reports any less fascinating, nor does it make them any less unnerving, especially, as in the case of a report from Worcester Way, when they involve a phantom child.

A van driver was out delivering fish one day when, out of nowhere, a child ran into the road. The driver hit his brakes hard but did not have time to avoid the child who ran straight into the path of his vehicle. When the van came to a halt the driver jumped out to tend to the child; to his amazement the child was nowhere to be seen. After checking all around the vehicle, he could find no trace of the child or of any damage to his van from the collision. The man concluded that he must have had a paranormal experience because, as he recalled later, the child he thought his van had struck appeared to have been wearing clothes that were not of the present era.

The Haunted Hotel

The Earl of Yarborough was the chairman of the Manchester, Sheffield and Lincolnshire Railway Company and also a very astute businessman. Recognising the fact that there would be an increase in trade in the town following the linking of the new railway line to the rail network, he built the Yarborough Hotel in 1851.

The most infamous period in the hotel's history occurred just eleven years later and became known as the Yarborough Riot. In February 1862, a fierce political battle was being fought between John Chapman and George Heneage. These were the days before the Reform Act, so both candidates for the election knew that every vote counted, and rumour had it that Heneage was bringing in two voters from Liverpool to boost his count.

On St Valentine's Day 1862, the day of the election, the two voters from Liverpool were met at the railway station by one of Mr Heneage's supporters and escorted to the Yarborough Hotel for refreshments. This meeting was witnessed by a local man who relayed the event to

Mr Chapman's supporters, who were, by now, fuelled by free alcohol and in a drunken rage.

Gathering on the opposite side of the street to the hotel, Chapman's mob then made their way across the road and congregated outside the Yarborough Hotel's entrance, where they demanded that the two out-voters show themselves. In an attempt to quell the mob Mr Stephens, the landlord of the Yarborough, allowed some of the men to enter the hotel and meet the two voters upstairs. After doing so, the men returned downstairs and left the building.

For a moment all seemed to have quietened down, then suddenly the hotel came under a barrage of stones and the enraged mob burst through the doors baying for the out-voters' blood. The entire Grimsby police force, which at the time only consisted of eight officers, did everything they could to try keep the peace and halt the rioters from making their way up the stairs to get to the two men, but they were soon overpowered.

Fortunately for the Grimsby policemen, there had been suspicions that there may be a problem on Election Day and between fifty and sixty officers from the Hull police force were also in Grimsby that day. The Hull officers were quick to assist their Grimsby colleagues in trying to clear the hotel as the incensed rioters attacked patrons and police officers, breaking windows and throwing furniture into the street. Within an hour, practically everything in the building was destroyed, but eventually the police managed to clear the rioters from the hotel and lock the doors; doors which had incidentally had their panels kicked in.

As the violence died down and the police gained control, sixteen rioters were taken into custody. They were tried at the Lincolnshire Summer Assizes on 30 July 1862. Four men were convicted of 'wounding, assaulting, beating and ill-treating their opponents and the police,' and sentenced to three months' hard labour in Lincoln prison.

As for the actual election, it was a close-run affair, with John Chapman polling 458 votes and George Heneage polling 446 votes.

Over a number of years, the hotel changed hands many times and strange occurrences began happening. Members of staff would report a feeling of unease in certain areas of the building. They would hear unaccountable noises and see figures in the shadows. Witnesses also reported seeing ghostly children in the hotel and encountered strange phenomena in the cellar. Customers were also beginning to report what appeared to be paranormal activity. The Yarborough's reputation for being haunted grew and, following an enquiry from a team of ghost hunters, the manager of the hotel at the time decided to allow them to investigate the building.

The P.P. Paranormal team from North Lincolnshire arrived at the Yarborough Hotel in 2009 and began their investigation. The team carried out a number of experiments in the building, including a séance and various vigils around the property. The most startling piece of evidence they captured during the evening appeared on a night-vision video camera. The footage, which was shot on a stairwell that leads down to the toilets, seems to show a figure appear from the left of the screen behind one of the investigators. It then moved behind him and virtually looked into the camera before it moved back out of shot to the left again. The figure, dressed in what appears to be

The Yarborough Hotel. (Photo courtesy of Kelly Day)

The Yarborough Hotel after the Election Day riot in 1862.

a shirt and tie and wearing glasses, looks very solid and almost too human not to be. The P.P. Paranormal team maintain that there was nobody other than the one team member in front of the camera at the time and that it would have been quite impossible for anybody to walk around behind him, as there was not enough room. The manager of the hotel was present at the time of the investigation and was wearing glasses, but he also maintained that he was standing behind the camera at the time the film was shot and that nobody who was involved in the investigation was wearing a white shirt. He also added, 'Nobody can explain exactly who this figure is that appears on the camera at that point.'

In 2010, workmen began fitting cables in the cellar of the hotel and part of the job involved knocking a wall down. As they began the demolition, the workmen noticed that there was a hidden room that had been sealed off behind the wall. There was nothing in the room and no indication as to what the room had been used for in the past. Perhaps a dark, secret history contained in the residual energy of the hidden room may have played a part in the cellar being one of the most paranormally active areas in the building.

Shortly after the work had begun in the cellar, another paranormal investigation at the Yarborough Hotel began. In September 2010, Lincolnshire Paranormal Investigators (LPI) were joined by Andrew Kilbee from the GRUB paranormal team. Together they held an overnight vigil at the building.

The team set up their equipment and began setting about their night's work. Andrew and another investigator headed for the cellar, whilst another team member remained at the top of the stair-way that leads down to the cellar. Whilst in the cellar, the investigators heard an unexpected noise. Something hit one of the barrels, making a 'ting' noise. The men were holding a vigil in darkness, so they didn't see who, or what, caused the noise. As neither of them had done anything to cause the noise, and they could find no natural explanation for the occurrence, they assumed that something had been thrown at the barrel, causing the sound. The investigator who was standing at the top of the stairs reported that nothing had past him during the incident, nor had he thrown anything into the cellar. Perhaps a spirit had been in the cellar with them and was trying to make its presence known.

The team went back upstairs to further investigate the building. Whilst carrying out another vigil, a member of the LPI was using a piece of equipment known as the ghost radar. This controversial piece of equipment is believed, by some, to track the movements of a spirit and show their whereabouts as a dot on a radar screen. The equipment is seen as controversial by some investigators in the paranormal field as it is largely regarded as an unproven technology. That said, other paranormal investigators believe that using and testing new technology can only help research and investigation into the subject. During the vigil at the Yarborough Hotel, the investigators had also set up some motion detectors upstairs. Suddenly, a red dot appeared on the ghost-radar screen, signifying that there was a presence in the room. The radar indicated the presence was moving towards the investigators and was just behind the motion detectors. One of the team called out and asked the presence to continue to move towards them and walk

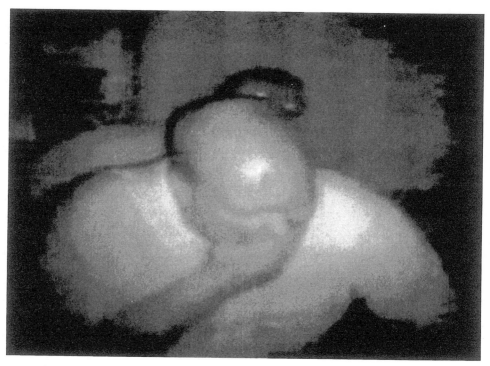

The Mysterious figure caught on video at the Yarborough Hotel by P.P. Paranormal investigators in 2009. (Photo taken from video footage by P.P. Paranormal; image remains copyright of P.P. Paranormanl)

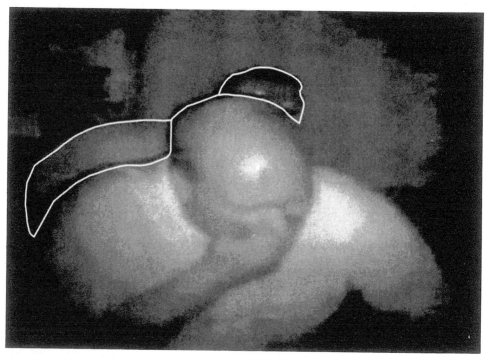

The unidentified figure is highlighted in white on this picture. (Photo taken from video footage by P.P. Paranormal; image remains copyright of P.P. Paranormanl)

electro-magnetic energy in a room in order to manifest itself, make a noise or move objects. An EMF meter measures the amount of electromagnetic energy in a room and a significant increase is believed, by some paranormal investigators, to be a sign that there is a spirit present. The investigator who was sitting in the bar at the Yarborough Hotel had a sudden increase in the EMF levels on his meter, or a 'spike' as it is known. He conveyed this to two other team members, who joined him at the table with their EMF meters. All three men put their meters down on the table and waited. Suddenly all three EMF meters began spiking for no apparent reason. They asked whoever was present in the room with them to stop the meters spiking; two seconds later the meters stopped and gave normal readings. They then asked the spirit to make the meters spike again and they did. Following this, the investigators began asking a series of 'yes or no' questions, using the response of the spikes in the meter readings to gauge the answers.

Lincolnshire Paranormal Investigators were joined by Andrew Kilbee from the GRUB paranormal team when they investigated the Yarborough Hotel in 2010. (Photo courtesy of Kelly Day)

The information they gleaned from this technique was that the spirit present in the Yarborough Hotel that evening was called Arthur. Arthur had not lived at the hotel and was not a regular patron. He said that he had committed a crime during his life but did not specify where or when.

into the motion detectors, this would break the beam in-between the detectors and set off an alarm. If this occurred it would add to the evidence that the building was haunted. After the investigator had called out to the spirit, the red dot on the radar moved in the opposite direction, as if it was backing away from the barriers and the team, until the dot disappeared from the radar screen completely. Maybe this ghost did not want the investigators tracking his movements so closely.

The team then moved their attention to the bar area of the hotel. One of the investigators sat at a table and turned on his EMF meter. The term EMF stands for electromagnetic field and there is a theory that a spirit will feed off the

The investigation team had all felt a presence that evening but nobody had felt like it was a malevolent one. They did all, however, have a feeling of guilt during their vigils, which perhaps they were picking up from the residual energy of the guilty spirit.

Was Arthur the same spirit that was allegedly captured in the video during the investigation at the hotel a year earlier?

Was his crime the part he played in the Yarborough Riot in 1862?

Was Arthur not a man, but indeed one of the ghostly children often witnessed at the Yarborough Hotel in the past?

Perhaps further investigations of the building in the future may provide more conclusive evidence as to the identity of the ghosts that haunt the hotel.

The Civil War Ghost

During the twentieth century, a rather unusual spectre was seen by a lady in Binbrook. The woman was walking along the verge of a road leading out of the village, when she saw what she believed to be the ghost of a Roundhead soldier. The figure wore the garb of a military man synonymous with those worn by the Parliamentarians, who fought on the side of Oliver Cromwell during the British Civil Wars of the 1600s.

Little more is known of this haunting or who this lost soul may be. A glimpse into historical accounts of the time tells us that during the Civil War in Lincolnshire, in 1643, the Parliamentarian forces were unable to hold out against Lord Newcastle's Royalist army, after initially gaining control of Gainsborough and Lincoln. Parliamentarian Commander, Lord Willoughby, eventually abandoned both Gainsborough and Lincoln and retreated to Boston, whilst the Royalist army headed back up north to Hull. The ghostly Roundhead could, therefore, be a soldier who lost his life during the skirmishes surrounding the retreat, or simply a lost soul trying to find his way back home.

The ghostly Roundhead that haunts Binbrook. (Illustration by Jason Day)

Terror on the Farm

A bizarre series of events occurred at Binbrook Farm, over a period of a month or so, in the early 1900s. Many claims were made in the press regarding the case and the cause of the phenomena that occurred at the property. Speculation on the cause ranged greatly, with everything from witchcraft to spontaneous human combustion, and even fraudulent claims of paranormal activity being cited by some. Given the time-frame of events and eyewitness reports from that period, it seems more likely that if some paranormal source was responsible for the occurrences, it is most likely to have been a poltergeist.

According to a report by Colonel Taylor of the Society for Psychical Research, the first instance of paranormal activity at the farm was reported by a Mrs White. On Friday, 30 December 1904, a milk pan was mysteriously overturned by an unseen force in the farmhouse kitchen. Throughout January 1905, the physical paranormal phenomena escalated in the house. Objects were thrown around the rooms and unaccountably fell from shelves. There were also instances of apports (the paranormal transference of an object from one place to another) within the building too. Small fires began breaking out for no apparent reason at the farmhouse. These fires were reported to occur near fireplaces where a 'not very good or big fire' would be burning in the hearth. The insinuation being that, although there was a source nearby, these mysterious fires could not have been ignited by them. Further evidence, which added weight to these claims, came from a letter published in the *Liverpool Echo*, which was sent in by a school teacher from Binbrook on 21 January 1905. The teacher claimed that one of the fires was caused by a blanket that spontaneously burst into flames; the blanket was found burning in a room where there was no fireplace. There are accounts of at least three of these mysterious fires during the month of January 1905. Although the paranormal activity in the farmhouse had been terrifying, it hadn't resulted in any physical injury to any member of the household or staff, but that was soon to change.

A servant girl was badly injured whilst working in the kitchen, and it was thought that the entity residing within the farmhouse may have been responsible. The following report was related by the farmer at Binbrook:

Our servant girl, whom we had taken from the workhouse, and who had neither kin nor friend in the world that she knows of, was sweeping the kitchen. There was a very small fire in the grate: there was a guard there, so that no one can come within two feet or more of the

A servant girl was badly burned in an alleged poltergeist attack at Binbrook Farm in 1905.
(Illustration courtesy of Tracie Wayling)

fire, and she was at the other end of the room, and had not been near. I suddenly came into the kitchen, and there she was sweeping away, while the back of her dress was afire. She looked around, as I shouted, and, seeing the flames, rushed through the door. She tripped, and I smothered the fire out with wet sacks. But she was terribly burned, and she is at the Louth Hospital, now, in terrible pain.

Records show that the girl was indeed admitted to Louth Hospital with extensive burns to her back and was in a critical condition. She maintained that she was in the middle of the room when her dress ignited. With the severity of her injuries, it would appear that the servant girl was on fire for a considerable amount of time. With the immediate action taken by the farmer to smother out the fire and the absence of her screaming out in pain, or indeed for help, before the farmer came to her assistance, it would appear that she must have been unaware of whatever was burning her at the time of the accident.

The unexplained movement of objects and spontaneous outbreaks of fires are both common factors in poltergeist cases. Another common factor in poltergeist cases is the involvement of a young girl. Young girls are often the focus of the activity and the servant girl involved in this case may very well have been the source from which the entity derived its energy. Admittedly, people are seldom injured by the fires, let alone set on fire in such cases, but the Binbrook Farm poltergeist case seems to be a very unique and violent one. As the paranormal activity spread to the out-buildings and grounds of the farm, the conduct of the entity became even more ferocious.

A labourer on the farm tethered a pair of horses to a wagon in a shed, ready to lead them out. As he attempted to move the wagon, the horses moved forward but the wagon remained rooted to the spot. He added a further two horses to the wagon and still it would not budge. A further four horses were tethered, bringing the total to eight, and still the wagon was immovable. The farmhand summoned several of his colleagues, who were just as perplexed as to why eight powerful horses would prove an insufficient force to move it. Convinced that the invisible agency that was plaguing the farm was at work, the farmhands summoned the farm foreman. The foreman entered the shed and ordered the farmhands to join the effort and begin pushing the wagon whilst the horses pulled it. He then sat in a wheelbarrow and observed the proceedings. As the farmhands attempted to push the cart, the wheelbarrow and the foreman were suddenly and inexplicably wheeled along at great speed by unseen hands. The farmhands fled the shed and left the foreman, wheelbarrow, horses and wagon to their own devices.

The most disturbing and unusual aspect of the Binbrook Farm case also occurred outside of the farmhouse and involved some of the farm's livestock. During the haunting, something began killing the chickens on the farm and an explanation for the bizarre nature of the deaths has never been found. The farmer, Mr White, claimed that during January 1905, from a total of 250 fowl on the farm only twenty-four survived. He explained:

They have all been killed in the same weird way. The skin around the neck, from the head to the breast, has been pulled off, and the windpipe drawn from its place and snapped. The fowl house has been watched night and day, and, whenever examined, four or five birds would be found dead.

In early February 1905, the paranormal activity at the farm dissipated and then, as suddenly as it had stared, it stopped. What sets the Binbrook Farm haunting apart from most other poltergeist cases is the sheer scale of the violence involved. There have been other cases where people are hit, slapped, scratched and even worse, but surely a case where somebody may have actually been set on fire by an entity, which may then have also killed 226 birds by literally tearing their throats out, must rank as one of the most horrific and terrifying poltergeist infestations on record.

The Lost Souls of Binbrook

RAF Binbrook was opened in June 1940, housing No.1 Group, Bomber Command. It was a front-line bomber station throughout the war, housing Nos 12 and 142 squadrons and No.460 squadron, Royal Australian Air Force. After the war, the airfield remained open, and during the early post-war period housed Nos 12, 9, 101 and 617 squadrons. The base closed in 1988 when the Lightning aircraft were retired from service. Once alive with the roar of jet engines, the runways have now been torn up; the station headquarters, guard rooms and barracks linger on in various states of decay and the former officers' mess shows signs of heavy vandalism and abandonment. The five large hangars that were once parts of RAF Binbrook now serve as storage facilities, and the housing complex has been turned into a village called Brookenby.

Like many bases, Binbrook saw its fair share of loss and tragedy during the war. On a December evening, four aircraft that were a part of No.460 squadron were returning from a raid in Berlin, when one of them crashed just short of the runway

Despite the attempts of many farmhands, a horse-drawn cart was rooted to the spot by the Binbrook Farm poltergeist. *(Illustration courtesy of Tracie Wayling)*

at the base, due to the weather conditions. Another disaster occurred on the evening of 3 July 1943, when an electrical short circuit on Lancaster DV172 caused the entire bomb load to drop to the ground. Within minutes, the 4,000lb 'Cookie' and two 500lb bombs exploded and the bomber disintegrated. Many witnesses believe that these, and other horrific incidents at the base, led to Binbrook becoming one of the most haunted locations in Lincolnshire.

Sightings of ghostly apparitions began at Binbrook towards the latter part of the Second World War. People started to report seeing what looked like a phantom airman standing at the end of the main runway. He was frantically jumping up and down and signalling to an aircraft at the end of the track. Yet there was no aircraft there. The pilot is believed to be a deceased sergeant who was part of the base's ground crew. He was in charge of loading a bomber before take off and only after the bomb load had been put into the bomb bay did he realise that the bombs had been armed. His spirit is said to have been seen on several occasions waving his arms at the unseen Lancaster bomber that is waiting to take off with armed bombs, trying to warn the crew.

Further apparitions were seen around the buildings on the complex during its days of active service. One of the blocks at the base was haunted by the ghost of a serviceman who had been killed in an accident. When this apparition materialised, witnesses reported that he could only be seen from the shins upwards. His ghostly amputation was accounted for by the fact that the first floor had been raised

by 6in since the haunting began. Another spirit that was seen frequently was that of a WRAF officer. She was often seen riding a bicycle towards the squadron headquarters building before vanishing as startled witnesses looked on. Other serviceman told of finding a stranger looking through the contents of the wardrobes in their living quarters. When the man was challenged he simply disappeared.

During the mid-1970s, an airman was returning to work after a late supper break. He was walking along a path between a storage building and a shed when he spotted a warrant officer walking from behind the shed. Not wanting to be seen by the officer in a state of disarray,

The phantom airman seen signalling non-existent aircraft on the runway at RAF Binbrook. (Illustration courtesy of Tracie Wayling)

The spectral WRAF officer seen cycling around the grounds of the base at RAF Binbrook.
(Illustration courtesy of Tracie Wayling)

the airman straightened up his dishevelled uniform and adjusted his beret. As he approached the officer he said, 'Good evening Sir,' but got no reply. He continued his journey and arrived at his work station. As he carried out his duties, the airman recounted his journey to work, mentioning how he had managed to avoid a scalding from the warrant officer by smartening himself up before he saw him. A sergeant overheard the airman and asked him to describe what the warrant officer looked like. The airman gave his sergeant a description of the man and the sergeant's demeanour changed immediately. The sergeant told him, in no uncertain terms, not to be so ridiculous, as the warrant officer he had described had died two days previously. The airman, who was known as something of a 'hard man' by his colleagues, fainted on the spot.

Other paranormal activity has also been reported at the location, including the sound of footsteps on the roof of Block 3 during the day and night. There was also unexplained activity in the 'bomb dump', where there were problems with lights being switched on and off of their own accord. The sound of switches being flicked on in sequence was heard, but never the sound of the footsteps of someone walking the corridor in order to switch them on. Armourers, on overnight 'sleeping-in' duty in the dump, would often describe being woken by the continuous ringing of the gate bell and the rattling of the chained and padlocked gates.

A further anomaly was reported in the base's hangars. During the night, mysterious phone calls were being made to the guardroom from phones within the hangars. Every time the guards answered the phone they would be met with silence.

When they went to investigate the source of the call, they would find the telephone handsets in their correct positions. This may not sound unusual, as it could have been 'prank' calls and the 'prankster' could have put the receiver back and left before the guards got there. The unusual thing about some of these calls were the occasions when the guard in the guardroom heard (over the phone line) the rattling of the hangar doors as his colleague left the room he had just checked, even though the phone receiver at the other end was in its correct position on the phone at the time.

Some servicemen at the base believed that the spirit responsible for some of the physical paranormal activity could be a corporal who served there and who took his own life by hanging himself from a bunk bed.

Perhaps the most infamous ghost at the former RAF Binbrook is that of a rather angry Australian airman, who had the rather unfortunate nickname of 'Clubfoot'. The airman was an NCO armourer at the base during the Second World War, and he was unfortunately injured due to the carelessness of a pilot. This resulted in the injury that earned him the cruel nickname he was given. Following his recovery, 'Clubfoot' continued to work at the base and embarked upon a plan of revenge. He attempted to sabotage the Lancaster Bomber aircraft that the pilot who had caused his injury was to due fly. Tragically, his plan went horribly wrong, as the explosive device he was attempting to attach to the aircraft's bomb load activated, and he was killed by an explosion of his own making. The ghost of 'Clubfoot' was seen regularly for many years, limping along the perimeter road of the base, and is still seen occasionally today. Some say he may even be the phantom that is seen attempting to flag down vehicles in the area.

The Curse of Cadeby Hall

Legend has it that many years ago, the body of a young boy was found in woodland close to Cadeby Hall. Upon hearing the news of the loss of her child, the boy's mother is said to have cursed the building and its occupants. Some would say the legendary curse may be more fact than fiction, given the history of the building, its location and those that have lived, and died, there.

The hall stands in the long deserted village of Cadeby near Beesby. Little is known of when or how the village became a ghost town, but there are suggestions that this could have happened during the Black Death of the medieval period. There are also suggestions that the desertion of the area may have been for purely economic reasons.

Cadeby Hall has seen a succession of owners, frequently changing hands over the years. In fact, one change of ownership actually took place over a game of cards when, in the late 1600s, the owner of the estate, Hugh Hammersly (the vicar of Roxby), lost the hall to a member of the Pelham family after being dealt a losing hand. The hall also fell into various states of disrepair over the years.

Tragedy beset the hall in 1885, when a young boy called George Nelson, who lived at the hall at the time was thrown from his horse and died. His family erected a memorial stone for George, marking the spot where his body was found. Originally the stone was in a grass field, more or less towards the centre.

When the field was turned to arable land, sometime after the 1960s, the stone was moved to its present location in a dyke bank on the east side of the A18, between Cadeby and Wyham Bends.

In 1986, Cadeby Hall was listed as 'at risk' and 'partially derelict'. The building was finally saved when it was restored in the first decade of the 2000s and is currently a private family home.

The hall is also said to have a haunted history that rivals the curse itself. A phantom coach and horses is reputed to proceed up the driveway to the house, signalling the imminent death of a resident of the hall. A spectral coachman disembarks the coach and knocks at the door. He then disappears as the door is answered. The phantom is said to call during the evening and a member of the household is found dead the following day.

There have also been sightings of ghostly monks in the grounds of the hall, and a mysterious blue lady has reputedly been seen in one of the bedrooms.

Cadeby's most famous spirit must surely be that of George Nelson himself. The ghost of George Nelson has been seen galloping along the road where his memorial now stands, on the A18 between Cadeby and Wyham. The phantom horseman rides out in front of unsuspecting motorists, who have attested to slamming on their brakes, certain that they have hit the rider and his steed, only to find that when they get out of the vehicle to assist, that the horse and rider have vanished.

A phantom coach, complete with horses, was said to be a portent of death when seen at Cadeby Hall.
(Illustration by Jason Day)

The ghost of George Nelson, Cadeby Hall's most famous ghost. (Illustration courtesy of Tracie Wayling)

Hell Hounds

A 'Black Dog' or 'Shuck' is the name given to a creature found primarily in the folklores of the British Isles. The Black Dog is essentially a nocturnal apparition, often said to be associated with the Devil; a 'hell hound' if you will. Black Dogs and Shucks are also sometimes referred to as 'Doom Dogs'. It is said that their appearance bodes ill for the beholder, although not always. More often than not, stories tell of Black Dogs terrifying their victims, but leaving them alone to continue living normal lives. In some cases it has supposedly happened before close relatives of the observer become ill or die. Black Dogs are almost universally regarded as malevolent, even to the extent that their appearance is regarded as a portent of death to the witnesses themselves. A few (such as the Barghest) are even said to be directly harmful, attacking their victims on sight. This association seems to be due to the scavenging habits of dogs. It is possible

A Shuck. (Illustration by Jason Day)

that the Black Dog is somehow a survival of these beliefs. Some, however, like the Gurt Dog in Somerset and the Black Dog of the Hanging Hills, are said to behave benevolently. According to folklore, these spectres often haunt graveyards, side-roads, crossroads and dark forests.

One such hound is said to haunt St Anthony's Bank in Cleethorpes. The beast has been seen on several occasions by terrified witnesses in the area.

An interesting off-shoot of the Black Shuck legend is the phenomena of the White Shuck. These creatures have all the same attributes of a Black Shuck, only they are white in colour. There have been reported White Shuck sightings in Little Cawthorpe and Haugham, near Louth.

The Child in the Water

Chapman's Pond is a large, natural expanse of water in Cleethorpes. The pond is surrounded by Cleethorpes railway line on the eastern side, an industrial estate on the southern side and two housing estates on the northern and western sides.

The pond has not always been there; in fact, it was originally opened as a brick pit in 1881. When excavation work began, the area was treated as two separate pits, eventually being merged into one large pit. In 1904, the workmen accidentally hit a freshwater spring and were unable to stem the flow of water; a steam-engine pump was brought in to lower the water level. The pit remained in service for a further eleven years, during which time it gradually continued to fill with water and required constant pumping. The pit was closed down in 1915 because of fears that light from the fires of the clay kilns in the pit would attract the attention of German Zeppelins during wartime.

Prior to the days of computer games, iPods and indeed television, many children would play outdoors. They would play ball games, ride bikes, fish and look for places to explore. Chapman's Pond was an ideal place for children during these times. They would play there, go fishing with their homemade rods and nets or even swim. The problem was, as enticing an environment as it was for the children to play in, the pond was also a very dangerous place too. Unfortunately, not every child who set out on an adventure to Chapman's Pond returned home. Several have lost their lives by drowning in its unforgiving waters over the years.

There is a local story that a man accidentally drove his horse and carriage into the pond one night, and that both he and his steed perished. They are said to haunt the area, but others believe it is just legend and superstition. It is worth bearing in mind though that this mode of transport was still in use until as late as the 1950s, especially for transporting goods. So it is not impossible that such an accident could have occurred.

Another poor soul, who is said to haunt the pond, makes their presence known in a much more dramatic fashion. Several independent eyewitnesses have reported seeing a young girl splashing around in the water and screaming for help. Whilst the witnesses go to fetch help and raise the alarm, she vanishes without a trace. Other reports claim that when attempts have been made to physically rescue the girl, she has vanished before the witness' very eyes. Although it is impossible to definitely identify the girl, it is believed that she is the spirit of one of the poor children who lost their lives in the pond.

The Playful Child

Cleethorpes Railway Station was opened in 1863 and has taken countless passengers to and from the seaside resort over the years. Many of which were holiday makers and day-trippers, especially around the turn of the nineteenth and twentieth centuries.

One such group was a large number of Sunday School children from Conisbrough, who visited Cleethorpes on an excursion in July 1900. They had enjoyed their annual school trip to the seaside and had returned to Cleethorpes Railway Station to catch the train home. Eleven-year-old Lizzie Williams waited on the platform with her thirteen-year-old sister and the other children. There were also several teachers and railway staff on the crowded platform, who were all waiting for the train that was due to arrive at 7.20 p.m. As they waited, a heavy shower set-in over the uncovered platform and everybody was anxious to get out of the rain.

According to Tom Justice, the assistant guard on the train in question, the train had drawn out of one of the sidings in the direction of Grimsby, for the purpose of backing into the station, into position for departure. Tom was standing on the step of the rear of the brake and as the train came alongside the platform, he tried to keep the people clear. He called out to the passengers to stand back and keep clear. He then moved from the brake step onto the platform and continued in his endeavours to keep the children clear of the train. The train continued to back in to the platform at a speed of around 4 mph.

As the crowd of drenched passengers noticed the train pulling in, they jostled

Cleethorpes Railway Station platforms.
(Photo courtesy of Kelly Day)

and hustled to board the slowly moving train and escape the weather. Lizzie Williams was carried along with the crowd and fell from the platform.

Tom Justice saw Lizzie fall from the platform halfway down the platform and halfway along the train. Upon hearing her scream, he immediately called out, 'Stop the train at once,' and the driver pulled up within the length of two coaches. The train was about 50 yards from the proper position for pulling completely into the station. Justice ran without delay to assist Lizzie, who was lying between the platform wall and the train; she had been severely crushed. Dr Savery, from Cleethorpes, was in attendance within ten minutes, and accompanied her to the hospital where he assisted Dr Champion

in trying to save her. Sadly, Lizzie Williams died from her injuries at 1:30 a.m. the following morning.

From witness testimony over the years, it is thought the little girl from Conisbrough may be the spirit that is believed to have haunted the station during the early part of the twentieth century. There were reports that, whilst waiting on the platform, some passengers could hear the sound of a child's voice whispering, and, in some instances even had their clothing tugged. There were also reports of people sensing that there was someone, or something, close to them, even when the station seemed to be deserted. Perhaps Lizzie was being mischievous in the way that children do when they want to play.

There were no actual sightings of the little girl, so it is not possible to say for sure if it was Lizzie. As reports of paranormal activity in the station have waned over the years, we may never find out either. Maybe Lizzie, if she was haunting the station, has been able to move on. It just may be worthwhile to keep your eyes and ears open next time you are waiting for a train at Cleethorpes Station though, you never know!

Fairground Spooks

Wonderland in Cleethorpes, situated at the end of the resort's North Promenade, began life as an amusement park arcade. As early as the 1920s, a galloping horse ride stood outside the building, in the area that is now a car park. Throughout its life as a leisure venue, Wonderland passed through several owners including Sam Brumby, The Smiths and the Felcey brothers. By 1965, the galloping horses had trotted inside the building and Wonderland had become an indoor venue. Five years later, the Felceys sold Wonderland to Mr Dudley Bowers, who continued to run the venture as an indoor fairground. Wonderland persisted to entertain the public with carousels, games of chance and even its very own ghost train. By 1981, the galloping horses had been put out to pasture (i.e. sold to a Dr Pandora Moorhead) and the writing was on the wall for Wonderland as an amusement venue. Bowers shut down the amusements and turned the building into an indoor market of the same name. Wonderland indoor market was once famed as one of the busiest around, attracting tourists and residents alike. In 2005, the building was sold by Bowers to Town and Country Markets. Sadly, in recent times, the building has become somewhat disused, and trade has fallen, sparking fears its best days are over.

The chequered history of Wonderland, and the many characters that have passed in and out of its doors, should make this building a prime candidate to be haunted, and indeed they do. Not only does the building house the happy memories of those that visited the fairground there, it is also home to some rather dark and tragic memories too. Some would even go as far as to say that these memories appear to be kept alive from beyond the grave, by the very souls that are fated to live them over, time and time again.

One of the apparitions, seen frequently within the building, is said to be that of Ruben Felcey. Ruben was one of the Felcey brothers that owned the building in the mid-1900s. Ruben saw mixed

Wonderland indoor market, Cleethorpes. (Photo courtesy of Kelly Day)

A young girl who tragically lost her life is said to haunt Wonderland. (Illustration courtesy of Tracie Wayling)

fortunes within his time at Wonderland, having owned the building during its heyday and also (it is said) when his son took his own life in the building. Various members of staff believe they have encountered the ghost of Ruben Felcey at one time or another, claiming that he is one of the elderly gentlemen that haunt the building. On one occasion, a witness saw a man get out of a vintage car and walk into the accounts office of the building. When the witness went into the office to see who the visitor was, and what he wanted, the man had vanished. Two other witnesses claimed to have seen the same figure leaning over a car bonnet on a different occasion. When they walked over to address the man, he disappeared into thin air.

A more tragic figure seen in the building is that of a small girl. She is believed to have been involved in a horrific fatal accident whilst on a ride at Wonderland, during its fairground days. Terrified witnesses have reported seeing the apparition of the little girl in the centre of the building where the ride used to be situated. What makes the sightings of this poor girl even more disturbing, is that she is seen as she was at the time of the accident, holding a bag and wearing a bloodstained dress.

Perhaps Wonderland's most infamous phantom is that of the old man known as Mr Poll. Mr Poll is believed to haunt the area that once housed the ghost-train ride. Stallholders, who rent pitches in the area, often remark on how unusually cold it is compared to the rest of the building. Witnesses, including staff and visitors to the building, have also reported hearing their names being called; even though there is nobody else around who knows them. Former owner of Wonderland,

Wonderland is said to be haunted by at least three spirits.
(Photo courtesy of Kelly Day)

Dudley Bowers, also reported an encounter with the spirit that is believed to be Mr Poll. Much like other eyewitness reports, Bowers saw the apparition of an old man who simply vanished before his very eyes.

According to local legend, Mr Poll was a lonely old man who would hang around the exit of the ghost train. Poll would offer sweets to the frightened children as they left the scary ride. Even though Mr Poll was not considered a threat to the children, concerned parents complained about his potential motives and he was banned from the area. Sometime later, the despondent Poll returned to Wonderland and was found hanging inside the entrance to the ghost train, having taken his own life.

The area believed to be haunted by Mr Poll.
(Photo courtesy of Kelly Day)

The Phantom Jumper

As is the nature of the subject, sometimes reported hauntings become based on a mixture of fact and fiction. Over time, these segue into folklore, and their origins, and sometimes their validity, are left open to question. This appears to be the case with the alleged haunting of an old water tower in Cleethorpes.

The water tower is a well-known landmark in the area and overlooks Chapman's Pond on the north-west side of Pelham Road. Fifty years ago, the tower was a far more grandiose sight, protruding from a sea of trees and dominating the skyline. Today, the tower has been absorbed into the Unifab Engineering Company on Pelham Road. The premises encroach onto land that was formerly part of the pond area. Over the years, the tower has also acquired a new cap and is significantly shorter than it was originally.

The origins of the haunting have been lost over time and eyewitness reports are now few and far between. Legend has it that in the past, there have been several sightings of a shadowy figure standing atop the tower. After pausing for a moment, the figure has then been seen to leap from the tower, only to disappear before hitting the ground. The details of who this tragic spirit may have been are open to debate. Was it somebody who had decided to take their own life? Was the fall the result of a tragic accident, or a prank that went horribly wrong? Or were there more sinister circumstances behind this event?

Since the industrialisation of the area surrounding the tower, sightings of the phantom jumper have been few and far between. Unfortunately, without new evidence to support the story, it is becoming increasingly regarded as folklore and urban legend.

The Girl that Proved Herself

The Lifeboat Hotel, located on the seafront in Cleethorpes, was reputed to be haunted by the ghost of a little girl. Members of staff reported feeling the presence of a spirit-child and encountering various unexplained phenomena during their shifts in the building. Customers at the hotel were not as convinced, especially the patrons that frequented the bar. Many of them believed that the mainly female staff were easily 'spooked' and were overreacting to the 'haunting legend' that had been passed down over the years, especially as

The Pelham Road water tower, Cleethorpes.
(Photo courtesy of Kelly Day)

nobody had claimed to have actually seen the girl.

One such sceptical customer was chatting with a friend in the bar of the hotel one evening, enjoying a quiet drink. Hearing an unusual noise behind him, both he and his friend turned to witness an ashtray, that was sitting on top of the cigarette machine, move slowly from one side of the machine to the other. The men looked at each other to confirm that they had both seen the same thing and then walked over to the cigarette machine to investigate.

The men tried to recreate what they had just seen, shoving the heavy pot ashtray across the top of the cigarette machine, but they could only manage to move it halfway across the machine. The machine was, as one of the men described it, a 'hefty piece of kit' and so would have been hard to move with a shove or vibration in order to make the ashtray glide across the top. The top of the machine was also very sticky with the remnants of spilled drinks, making it even harder to slide the ashtray across it. There was nobody near the machine when the inci-

The shy spirit of the Lifeboat Hotel.
(Illustration by Jason Day)

dent occurred and taking into account all of the elements involved, and their failure to recreate the event, the men decided they could come up with no rational explanation for the ashtray moving across the top of the machine. They decided it must have been the ghost of the little girl, proving she really was in the hotel, and so they toasted her with their next drink.

The Lifeboat Hotel has since been demolished and replaced with a block of flats on Queen's Parade that overlook the beach. Whether the spirit of the little girl will make her presence known to visitors to the new building or not remains to be seen.

The Ghost Train

The Bardney to Louth railway line was built in stages, beginning in 1874. The final stage, between Donington on Bain and Louth via Withcall and Hallington, opened to goods on the 28 June 1876 and to passengers on the 1 December 1876. A 48ft (15m) turntable was constructed at Bardney, to turn the engines working on the branch. Passenger services ended on the 5 November 1951 and goods traffic was discontinued in stages over the next ten years. The final section between Wragby and Bardney closed on the 1 February 1960, bringing to a close eighty-six years of railway history.

Although the track has been removed and a train has not passed along the line in over fifty years, locals from nearby Hallington claim to regularly hear the unmistakeable sound of a steam train passing along the old line in the stillness of the night.

A Haunting Habit

Humberston Abbey was founded during the reign of Henry II, probably around 1160, by William FitzRalph, a local landholder. The abbey is believed to have been constructed on an earlier Christian site, as examples of Anglo-Saxon carved stonework, from the mid-tenth to early eleventh century, are built into the walls of nearby St Peter's Church. Dedicated to St Mary and St Peter, the abbey was a house of the Tironian Order, a reformed branch of the Benedictines. It was never a large or rich establishment and is thought to have only housed a dozen monks at most. Badly damaged by fire in 1226 and 1305, fourteenth and fifteenth century records note many disagreements between the monks, and lapses in discipline. The house was one of the first to be suppressed by Henry VIII, at which time the annual income was £34, supporting an abbot, four monks and a lay-brother. Most of the abbey buildings were demolished by 1562, with the western end of the abbey church retained as a parish church. Apart from the fifteenth century tower, the church, now just dedicated to St Peter, was rebuilt between 1720 and 1722.

Following the Dissolution of the Monasteries, a manor house, recorded as Abbey House in 1708, was built on a raised platform to the south of the original abbey buildings. This was later demolished and replaced by the current house, closer to the church in the late eighteenth or early nineteenth century. The only remaining traces of the abbey are ground workings, including the 'monks' mound', a prominent feature in the manor-house garden.

During the 1900s, there were reports of an unexplained light floating across the ceiling of one of the bedrooms at the manor house. There were also mysterious banging sounds emanating from around the building. The phantom believed to be responsible for the paranormal activity is apparently the spirit of a former monk who was killed for breaking his vows.

The Ghost of Rosamund Avy

The small village of Irby has a population of 124 (according to the 2001 census) and is situated just south-west of Laceby. Over 550 years ago, a tragic event, filled with mystery and intrigue, shook the tiny village and it continues to manifest itself in a series of ghostly sightings.

One November night in 1455, Rosamund Avy and her fiancé were taking a walk in the woodland near Irby Top. The couple were due to be married the following day and were embarking on a romantic evening stroll. That evening, villagers in Irby heard terrifying screams from the woodland, and by the following morning neither Rosamund nor her future husband had returned. Two years passed and the locals had come to terms with the disappearance, but there were to be further developments. Rosamund's intended husband returned to the village and tongues began wagging. He told the people that, on this night he and Rosamund had quarrelled whilst out walking and he had assumed that she had returned home. With no evidence of any foul play, and Rosamund still missing, there was no proof that any crime had been committed and her former fiancé was never charged with any offence.

Rumours continued to spread around the village and, with no sign of Rosamund ever returning, coupled with the screams

The ghost of Rosamund Avy. (Illustration by Jason Day)

that had been heard on the night of her disappearance, many believed that she had been murdered. Some years later, the rumours seem to have had a little more substance to them, as workmen unearthed some bones in the area that were confirmed to be those of a young woman.

Over the years, the ghostly form of a young woman has regularly been seen in the woods, and as it has been seen more often than not on the anniversary of Rosamund's disappearance, the apparition is believed to be that of Rosamund Avy. Local people, who take regular walks in the area of her disappearance, have reported experiencing paranormal phenomena that they claim made them 'jump out of our skin'. These include unexplained noises and even being tapped on the shoulder by an unseen force.

One recent account came from a woman from Grimsby, who was out walking on Irby Top. The woman regularly walks in the area and knows the woods well. On the 5 May 2010, she was walking with a partner when they heard a loud whooshing sound behind them. They turned around and felt something pass between them. Maybe the unfortunate spirit of Rosamund Avy is trying to let somebody know what happened to her that night from the afterlife.

The Ghostly Hitchhiker

RAF Kelstern was situated around 6 miles north-west of Louth. The base was established in 1917 as a night landing ground for No.33 squadron RFC, to cater for any fuel emergencies during their Zeppelin hunts in the First World War. It closed again in 1919. In July 1942, further construction on RAF Kelstern commenced half a mile to the north-east of the landing ground. In September 1943 it opened once again, this time as No.12 Base substation and home to the No.625 squadron. The base was also occupied by No.170 squadron from October 1944 until its closure in May 1945. RAF Kelstern is now commemorated in a small memorial stone to No.625 squadron at the corner of the road, near the old airfield.

There have been many reports from the surrounding area of the sounds of unseen Rolls Royce Merlin aircraft engines running, both in the skies and along the former runways. The most shocking eyewitness testimony comes from those who claim to have seen Kelstern's phantom airman. The spectral pilot is described as wearing an old RAF uniform and carries a kitbag bearing one blue band. He has been seen on several occasions, since 1983, at various points along the road leading to the former base, trying to hitch a lift from passing motorists.

Road Ghosts of Louth

Road ghosts are one of the most commonly witnessed apparitions around the world and there is no shortage of them in and around the Grimsby area, particularly in Louth. One of the most common types of road ghost in the UK is that of the phantom coach and horses, so it should come as no surprise that Louth has a couple of these spectres of its own. One of which is the ghostly coachman of Oslear's Lane. This all but abandoned country lane, in the Maidenwell area of Louth, is home to a ghostly coach driver, who has been seen travelling at break-neck speeds along the lane. This is something he would find hard to do in the afterlife, as the terrifying apparition of the coach driver has neither a neck nor indeed a head.

Another staple of the British road ghost is that of the ghostly horse and rider. Barton Street, just north of Louth and south of Fotherby, is another lonely country lane. Many an unsuspecting driver, and pedestrian, has been startled by the sudden appearance of the phantom horse that is seen here throwing its rider from his saddle, before they both vanish.

The road leading into and out of Louth from the south is said to be haunted by a different type of phantom altogether, a phantom nun. She is often seen on the stretch of road between Little Cawthorpe and Muckton Bottom. Some eyewitnesses have seen the nun walking along the road; she proceeds straight

The Barton Street road ghost, thrown from his spectral mount in Louth. (Illustration by Jason Day)

through a boundary fence and into the plantation at Muckton. She is believed to be a residual haunting, carrying out the same journey she would have taken during her lifetime.

The London Road roundabout, where the B1520 from Louth meets the A16 and the A157, is the location for a more modern haunting, by road–ghost standards. A motorist at the roundabout witnessed what he described as a 'man riding an old-fashioned bike', cycling along the middle of the bypass. The motorist was in no doubt that what he saw was an apparition and described the man as wearing trousers, a jacket and a flat cap. From the man's appearance and the age of the bicycle he was riding, he deduced that he would date from around the turn of the twentieth century.

Spirit in the Attic

Sometimes you just don't know what your day is going to bring. Even if it just seems like a normal day at work, you never know – as was the case for a carpenter in Louth one day. The man made his way to Church Close and began what he thought was going to be a routine job in an attic room of a house.

He arrived at the house and set about his work in the attic room. Whilst he was working, the carpenter had the feeling that somebody had entered the room and was somewhere behind him. As he turned to acknowledge the person, he briefly saw a young girl in Victorian clothing sitting on the end of the bed. Before the startled man could speak, she vanished into thin air.

A spectral girl was seen by a workman in the attic room of a house on Church Close in Louth. (Illustration by Jason Day)

Accidentally on Purpose?

During the late 1990s, the Ghostbusters UK paranormal investigation team were called out to a case at a farm in Louth. The occupants of the farmhouse reported what they thought could be paranormal phenomena occurring in their home.

The witnesses told paranormal investigators that they had heard phantom footsteps and experienced unexplained cold spots in the farm buildings. They explained that the oppressive atmosphere at the location had become so intense that they felt a series of accidents at the site could be attributed to the haunting. Staff felt they had to act before things got any worse and so they brought paranormal investigators in to help.

Following their investigation of the site, the Ghostbusters UK team claimed to have removed the cause of the atmosphere and, it would seem, normality returned to Grange Farm.

The Hooded Entity, the Spectral Soldier and his Dog

Auguste Alphonse Pahud moved to Louth in 1875, to teach French and German at King Edward VI School. He met a wealthy farmer's daughter called Annie Grant and the couple soon fell in love. They married twelve years later and lived in The Limes, in Westgate. Auguste retired and the couple spent their time travelling extensively. Annie's health was not in a good state, so the couple decided to travel to the continent, hoping this would improve things. Unfortunately, whilst in London, in 1899, Annie died suddenly.

The couple had been inseparable over the years and the inconsolable Auguste became something of a hermit, until his death in July 1902.

In his £25,000 will, Auguste left instructions that a board of trustees should be set up to distribute his fortune, to celebrate the memory of his dear wife. The seven trustees invested £1,000 to fund a new window in Mrs Pahud's memory at the parish church. The Limes' building became a Girls' Grammar School and a fund was set up to assist the poor in the parish of Withern, where Annie's parents had farmed. It was agreed that Hubbard's Hillss, on the outskirts of the town, would be bought as a lasting memorial to Auguste's beloved wife.

The land was bought from the Lord of the Manor at Hallington, Mr J. Ward, for just over £2,000 – the sale included the lake and the watermill on Crowtree Lane. Improvements were made with extensive tree planting and the Hills were then given over to the people of Louth in 1907.

Less than a decade after Hubbard's Hillss became public land, a woman was walking her dog there when the terrier ran down a rabbit hole and disappeared. As she frantically tried to rescue her dog, a man walked by and asked her what she was doing. The woman told him and he tried to help her rescue the dog. Unfortunately, it could not be saved. The couple became friends and fell in love. The man was a Scottish soldier from Stirling and was in the Black Watch Regiment. In due course, the First World War began and he was called to the Western Front.

The soldier survived the war, including a German gas attack, and returned to Louth and his beloved. On his return, he brought her a new dog and the couple soon married and lived in Louth. The soldier outlived his bride and, much like Auguste Pahud, he never got over her death. The soldier passed away in his late ninities.

During the early 2000s, reports of paranormal activity on Hubbard's Hillss began coming in. There had been previous reports of unexplained phenomena in the area and sightings of apparitions, but these sightings were different. Witnesses were purporting to see the figure of a Scottish soldier in full uniform, walking with a dog at the top of the hill.

Animals were also being affected by the area. There are those, within the paranormal investigation fraternity, that believe animals are more sensitive to paranormal phenomena than humans. They believe that animals have a kind of 'sixth sense', which gives them an ability to know that spirits are near. Interestingly, when discussing the Hubbard's Hillss case with the local newspaper in 2003, Grimsby parapsychologist Robin Furman said, 'Dogs will not go past that spot, which seems to be about the place where the soldier met the Louth girl looking for her dog.'

Several dogs have also mysteriously disappeared in that area of Hubbard's Hillss, including one that was reported in 2002. The area has become so well known for its paranormal activity that both laymen and paranormal investigators have flocked to the Hills, to try and find evidence of a haunting for themselves.

On 18 April 2008, paranormal investigator Andrew Kilbee, and the Lincs Paranormal investigation team, travelled to Hubbard's Hillss to conduct an

Lincolnshire Paranormal Investigators believe they captured the image of a spirit in this photo taken at Hubbard's Hillss, Louth, in 2008. (Photo by Tony Hall and courtesy of Andrew Kilbee)

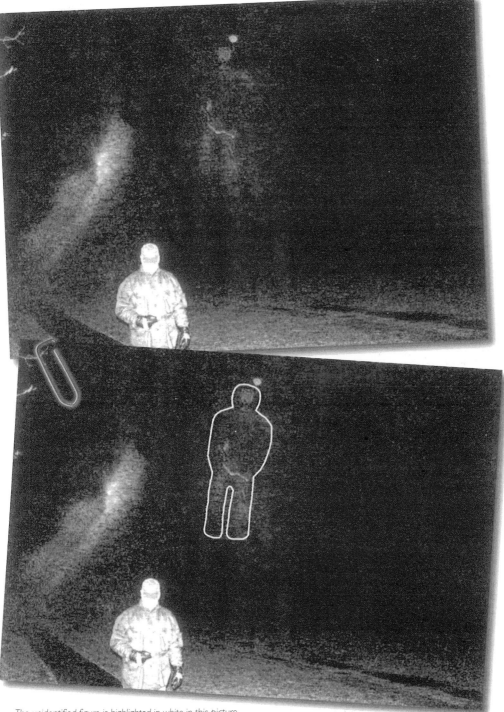

The unidentified figure is highlighted in white in this picture.
(Photo by Tony Hall and courtesy of Andrew Kilbee)

investigation of their own. Andrew was joined by Michael Evans, Paul Wilson and Tony Hall, and during the evening, the team conducted several experiments to try and detect any paranormal phenomena. After returning home to analyse their findings, the team discovered an interesting anomaly. Tony Hall had taken a photograph of Paul Wilson during the evening. Seconds before the picture was taken, Paul had sensed that there was somebody nearby and had asked Tony to take a photograph. The photo appeared to show the outline of a figure floating in mid-air above Paul. Could this have been the spirit of the soldier? Perhaps it was another individual that haunts the Hills.

Another paranormal investigation group, that have explored the location recently is Night Owls Paranormal, who are also based in North Lincolnshire. The founder members are paranormal investigator Steve Dinsdale and medium Suzan Drury. The team have investigated the sight on more than one occasion, but they too captured what they believed to be an interesting anomaly on camera. During their vigil at Hubbard's Hillss, on 25 September 2010, a photograph was taken near steps leading up a hill. What the team believe could be the silhouette of the head and shoulders of a hooded figure can be seen near the bottom of the steps. Further investigations will see if the team can get further corroborating evidence to support the photo.

Ghosts in Store

Not every disgruntled customer is 'of this world', according to some eyewitnesses who work in the retail industry. During the early twenty-first century, a shop, in the Upgate area of Louth, experienced unexplained wrappings on the walls of the building. Despite a thorough search of the location, no rational explanation could be found.

Another retailer, that has experienced physical paranormal phenomena is the Yorkshire Trading Company. In 2003, staff working in the Old Market Place in Louth witnessed a rail of shirts fly across the room with no apparent cause.

The Man in the Cape

Ye Old White Swan is a fourteenth-century pub, located on Eastgate in the heart of Louth. Like many pubs and inns, Ye Old White Swan is said to be haunted. Pubs are often the scene of great happiness or sorrow; some paranormal investigators believe that spirits use high levels of emotional energy, both bad and good, to materialise, so these buildings are an ideal location for apparitions to manifest themselves. Add to that the age of most pubs and the number of patrons that have passed through their doors, and it comes as no surprise that so many of these establishments are haunted.

Ye Old White Swan boasts a spectre that has been seen frequenting various areas of the building, usually before midnight. He is said to be unusually tall and wears a white cape. Although witnesses are obviously shocked after an encounter with the man, they say they have not felt threatened by him. This benevolent spirit may just be a former patron who fancies a pint at his favourite local.

Physical paranormal activity has also been reported at the building, one landlord heard pandemonium in an upstairs room. Hearing what he thought was the

The Night Owls Paranormal team caught what they believed to be a hooded figure on camera, during their 2010 vigil at Hubbard's Hillss, Louth. (Photo courtesy of Steve Dinsdale)

The unidentified figure is highlighted in white on this picture. (Photo courtesy of Steve Dinsdale)

sound of a crate of bottles crashing to the floor, he ran upstairs to investigate. Upon entering the room, he found that there was nothing on the floor. In fact, there were no crates, bottles or anything in the entire room that could have even fallen to the floor to make the noise he had heard.

Phantom Crossing

Mary Tomlinson-Harrison was stationed at RAF Manby between 1961 and 1963. It was during this period of time that she witnessed an extraordinary event that remains unexplained to this day.

One evening, Mary went to the local chip shop to get some supper. It was approximately 11 p.m. as she headed back to the barracks, approaching a level cross-ing. As she walked towards the gates of the crossing, she noticed they were open and in a bad state of repair. Suddenly the thunderous noise of a railway engine burst through the quiet of the night. Beyond the darkness, Mary saw what appeared to be a steam engine passing over the crossing, illuminated only by the fire of its engine. Terrified by the lack of lighting, the noise of the engine and danger of the open gates at the crossing, Mary stood rigid with fear. Meanwhile, the steam engine, complete with two carriages, passed in front of her and disappeared into the night. Once the train had gone, Mary fled back to the nearby safety of RAF Manby.

Upon her return, Mary was naturally showing the signs of her recent encounter. Seeing her in distress, a Sergeant in the guard room asked Mary if she

The ghost train witnessed during the 1960s in Louth. (Illustration courtesy of Tracie Wayling)

was ok and what had happened to her. Mary relayed the events of the evening to the sergeant, who was somewhat perplexed by what she said. The sergeant told her that nearby Grimoldby Railway Station had been closed for at least two years and the track had been lifted up for at least a quarter of a mile on either side of the level crossing.

Indeed, the sergeant was right. Mary's sighting occurred between 1961 and 1963. Grimoldby Station closed on the 5 December 1960 and the last train to ever run on the Louth to Salfleetby line – the line that crossed the level crossing – ran two days earlier on the 3 December 1960, putting Mary's sighting of the mysterious train anywhere between a month and up to three years after the line had closed.

An interesting side-note to this story is that Grimoldby Station was the childhood home of actor Donald Pleasance, whose father was the station master. Donald, of course, starred in such notable horror movies as *Circus of Horrors*, *Tales That Witness Madness* and the *Halloween* series of movies, amongst many others.

Ghosts of the Past

Construction of RAF Manby began on the site in 1936. From 1938, the special function of the airfield was as a base for No. 1 Air Armament School (from 1944, Empire Central Armament School), which was concerned with training in air gunnery and bomb-aiming skills. The actual ranges for these activities were at Thaddlethorpe. At some time during the Second World War, concrete runways were added.

In 1949, the Royal Air Force Flying College (later renamed the College of Air Warfare) was formed at Manby. In the 1960s, a new control tower and signals square were built, superseding the earlier pre-war tower. Many of the houses in the village were built as homes for RAF personnel, and the streets that house them are named after aeroplanes (e.g. Vampire Road). RAF Manby closed in 1974 and since the closure of the airfield, the houses have been sold to the general public and the former RAF station has been sold for commercial use.

The headquarters of East Lindsey District Council are now situated in one of the buildings on the station (Tedder Hall). The disused airfield has been used as a showground and is now an off-road driving centre, and one of the hangars is used as a grain store as part of the European Union Common Agricultural Policy. It also has a chieftain tank parked in the entrance to the airfield.

There have been many reports of paranormal phenomena in and around the area of the former base, dating as far back as the 1980s. For instance, a ghostly bag-piping airman has been seen, and heard, near the crossroads at RAF Manby, and the drone of spectral aircraft is often heard in the skies over the old runways. The figure of a Second World War pilot has also been seen in and around the area on several different occasions. Some witnesses describe his as wearing flying gear, and others as wearing a long coat.

Former RAF buildings have also been the scenes of unexplained occurrences according to some eyewitnesses. One member of staff, who worked for East Lindsey District Council, experienced such activity at Tedder Hall. The witness used to work a lot of hours on a Sunday,

Phantom Lancaster bombers have been seen over the skies of the former RAF facility in Manby. (Illustration by Jason Day)

as they found there was far less traffic on the roads and thus it was easier for them to get in and out of work, and therefore get more work done.

They reported that most of the time they were in the building alone on a Sunday. Their office at Tedder Hall overlooked the car park and the main gate, which the witness always locked once they were inside. On a number of occasions, the witness would hear office doors opening or footsteps in the hall, despite the fact that there was nobody else in the building. The witness recalled, 'The first time I heard it, it scared the bejeezers out of me, but after a while you got used to it.'

The Shopping Poltergeist

There are many reported incidents of poltergeist activity and the Spar shop, on Station Road in New Waltham, is one such location that has experienced this particular type of paranormal phenomena.

Several years ago, a witness began working at the store under its former owners, Tates. The witness was a naïve sixteen-year-old and was told by other members of staff that one morning they had come in to open the store, only to be greeted by something very peculiar. The staff found that, in every isle, there was a solitary line of tins that spanned the entire length of the isle. These tins had not been there when staff had locked the store up the previous evening and, to their knowledge, nobody had been in the shop overnight. They also told the witness that objects would often go missing and then reappear again without an explanation.

A little perturbed after hearing the spooky tales, the witness reassured herself that this was just the staff trying to scare a teenager embarking on their first job, and began work. During their time there, the witness never experienced any unexplained occurrence; that was until the time that a jam jar suddenly flew from a shelf and landed only 6ft away from them. There was nobody within 'throwing distance' of the witness at the time of the incident, nor was there any apparent 'natural cause' for the object to have been thrown from the shelf with such force. The closest person to the shelf was a butcher, who was standing behind a refrigerated glass display. The witness also recalled that the neighbouring premises, at the time, was a hairdressers and that both shops were at least 50ft from the road, to allow for a car park. This would surely rule out the cause of movement as vibration, and if it didn't, why didn't any of the other objects on the shelf move or fall from it?

The witness claimed that following these incidents, they learned that the store was built during the 1960s and the village post office once stood on the site. The former post master is said to have committed suicide by hanging himself at the location.

The witness left the store a fortnight later to pursue other employment avenues and was, therefore, unaware of any other paranormal activity following their own experience, which happened many years ago. Upon researching the case further, I found that the site was the home of the former village post office but, unfortunately, I have been unable to substantiate the story of the postmaster's death.

Poltergeist cases are usually short, violent outbursts of paranormal activity that come and go very quickly. Whether it is the spirit of the former post master, or another lost soul that caused the unexplained events at the Spar store, it will be interesting to see if any further incidents are reported in the future.

Dark Secrets Come to Light

St Botolph's Church is located in Skidbrooke, near Louth. The thirteenth-century building stands on marshland nestled amongst a clump of trees and weather-worn gravestones. Due to diminished attendances, the church has remained unused as a place of worship since its closure in 1973 – a fact that can be easily attested to when one sees the lack of windows, and interior furnishings, and the birds that are frequently found inside (complete with droppings and feathers covering the floor). St Botolph's is now under the care of the Churches Conservation Trust and has been the scene of much controversy over the past decade.

There are claims that the church, and its grounds, are amongst the most haunted spots in Lincolnshire, boasting a plethora of paranormal activity. These claims saw a spate of unwanted visitors arriving at the site during the early twenty-first century and not all of those were otherworldly.

In the summer of 2003, the Bassetlaw Ghost Research Group travelled from Retford to investigate the church. The team carried out several experiments, during their overnight vigil, using many different types of equipment to record their findings. They claimed to have captured up to 200 'rods' on their night-vision cameras. Rods are cylindrical objects that travel at very high speeds; they are often invisible to the human eye. As paranormal investigator David Wharmby explained to a reporter from the *Louth Leader* newspaper, 'They are about four inches to a foot in length and are not visible to the naked eye. They could be flying insects, aliens or something of a paranormal nature.'

The team also experienced feelings of unease and heard strange, unaccountable noises. Members of the group saw flashes of light in what was a clear sky and even maintained that they saw the apparitions of small children in amongst the grass and the gravestones.

With the nearest house sitting half a mile away from the haunted church, it was an ideally secluded location to conduct a paranormal investigation, but this also meant it was an ideal location for other, less welcome visitors.

The *Louth Leader* reported that in January 2004, there was evidence that devil worshippers had begun using the church for their own exploits. Pillars in the church had been marked with black signs and the altar itself was painted black. The words 'Carla and Amy sacrificed here' were also written on the side of the altar. One local resident claimed the devil worshippers painted names and symbols on stones, which they then laid in a circle on the floor of the church. Sometimes villagers would see as many as ten cars parked outside the building late at night.

There were also suggestions that animals were sacrificed in the church, with headless cockerels and sheep being found nearby. A nature reserve wildlife officer

Satanic rituals are believed to have been carried out at St Botolph's Church in Skidbrooke. Some paranormal researchers think this may have led to increased paranormal activity in the area. (Illustration by Jason Day)

attested to finding a headless chicken in a car park close to the location. The church warden at the time, Ralph Benton, told the *Louth Leader*:

> Satan worshipping has gone on. They come from Grimsby in the evenings, light fires and write symbols on the walls. I have gone to the church at three in the morning to try to move them on, but they swear at me so I don't like to go. I might get knifed.

Nine months after the news of the alleged devil worship at the site, Lincs Paranormal Research team announced that they would be investigating St Botolph's Church, in October 2004. Local residents had other ideas. On Halloween night, four Skidbrooke villagers held their own overnight vigil, protecting the church. The men blocked the church with their cars and stood guard, wearing fluorescent jackets and holding torches. One of the men claimed they had turned away more than thirty people that evening. This included a car packed with 'would be ghost hunters', which stopped outside the church. The men surrounded the car and the church warden, Ralph Benton, told the driver, 'Go away. You are not wanted here.'

The men succeeded in averting any ghost hunts or devil worship at the church that night and the Churches Conservation Trust said they planned to employ a security guard at St Botolph's.

These measures may have helped keep ghost hunters and devil worshippers away, but it appears to have had no effect on the spirits that dwell there. In fact, there have even been reports of further hauntings in the village itself. One resident asked a priest to bless her home because of the unexplained paranormal activity she was experiencing there. Perhaps the dark activities that went on in the church have served to escalate hauntings in the village. As one Skidbrooke resident proclaimed, 'People may think it's a load of nonsense, but there is such a thing as black magic and it's dangerous.'

The Green Lady

Thorpe Hall is a country house situated within the parish of South Elkington, within walking distance of the market town of Louth. Just beyond the grounds of the hall lies Hubbard's Hills. The hall was in the possession of the Bolle family for many years, and it is a member of that particular family that the legend of the Green Lady centres around.

John Bolle was born in 1560 and eventually became the owner of Thorpe Hall. He married his wife Elizabeth and embarked on a career in the military in 1592. Under the Earl of Essex, Bolle commanded troops at the taking of the castles of Donolong and Lifford in Ireland. The earl later appointed him the governor of Kinsale.

In 1596, Elizabeth I, fearing a Spanish invasion, sent an expeditionary force to forestall the attack. John Bolle, now a captain, was a part of this mission, again under the command of Essex (who was now Lord Essex) and Lord Howard. On 20 June, the force fought for fourteen hours, scoring a notable victory in Cadiz. The following day, Captain Bolle was assigned the charge of one of the prisoners who had been taken during the conflict at Cadiz. His prisoner's name was Donna Leonora Oviedo. By all accounts she was a lady of extraordinary beauty, and of distinguished family and great wealth. Bolle's kind treatment of her whilst in his captivity began to evoke feelings of gratitude from Donna, which ultimately turned into love. This resulted in her throwing her riches and her person at the feet of Captain Bolle. The gallant captain refused her offers, which included marriage, and released her.

Such was her infatuation with Bolle that upon his departure from Cadiz on 15 July, the devoted Spaniard sent, as presents to his wife, a profusion of jewels and other valuables. Amongst these treasures were a beautiful tapestry-bed, several casks full of plate, money and a portrait of Donna, painted as she was, dressed in green. The inconsolable lady retired to a nunnery, where she spent the remainder of her days in sorrow and seclusion.

This version of the story of the Green Lady became the subject of a ballad, which was subsequently published in Percy's *Reliques of Ancient English Poetry*, and which was called 'The Spanish Ladye's Love for An Englishman'.

I say *this* version because there is also a more romanticised version of the story, which says John Bolle was captured by the Spaniards and imprisoned in a dungeon following the conflict in Cadiz. In this story, it is Donna Leonora Oviedo that frees Bolle from his captors, although as in the original version of the story she falls in love with him and is rebutted. Donna then follows Bolle back to England and ends her own life in Thorpe Park Gardens.

Following his return to England, Bolle's bravery and gallantry were rewarded and he was duly knighted for his part in the Cadiz campaign. Sir John Bolle returned to Thorpe Hall in 1599 and was given a civic reception. He died on 3 November 1606 at his beloved Thorpe Hall, aged forty-six. He was buried in Haugh Church and a monument was erected in his honour. With his death, the only living memory of the Green Lady was lost, except for the ballad and the portrait that she had given him, which hung on a wall in Thorpe Hall.

Sir Charles Bolle, Sir John's son, felt that the portrait of the Green Lady had taken a life of its own. He would say that he felt that she was looking down upon him, as if her personality was actually breathing within the painting. He began to believe that, perhaps, the heart and spirit of Donna Leonora Oviedo had somehow travelled to Thorpe Hall to be with his deceased father.

Sir Charles' mother, Sir John's widow, Elizabeth, passed away in 1647 and, following her death, the rumours that Thorpe Hall was haunted increased. It was as if the spirit of the Green Lady felt

John Bolle, former owner of Thorpe Hall, South Elkington. (Illustration by Jason Day)

The haunted portrait of Donna Leonora Oviedo, the Green Lady of Thorpe Hall. (Illustration by Tracy Wayling)

more comfortable within the grounds, now that the wife of her unrequited love was no longer around. Sir Charles himself was so convinced that Donna was haunting the house, and making her presence felt, that he would have an extra place set at his table, just in case she chose to appear.

Many of the local people also believed that Thorpe Hall was haunted by the Green Lady, and that she would take her seat in a particular tree near the mansion every night. She was also seen drifting around the grounds on a regular basis.

Thorpe Hall stayed in the Bolle family's possession until the mid-1700s; the portrait of the Green Lady was sold in 1760. One might think that with both the portrait and the Bolle family no longer in Thorpe Hall, the haunting would cease and the spirit of the Green Lady would move on. However, it would seem not, as the ghost of the Green Lady was still being seen by residents of Louth in 1834. Reports stated she was occasionally seen walking about the grounds of Thorpe Hall at midnight. More recent sightings would suggest that she is forever fated to search for a love she can never have.

The Headless Airman

RAF Strubby was the most easterly of Lincolnshire's airfields, but it was already surplus to Bomber Command requirements when it opened in April 1944. It was, therefore, initially used by Coastal Command, which deployed No.144 squadron and No.404 squadron RCAF to RAF Strubby on anti-surface vessel missions. Over the next year, three more squadrons were housed at RAF Strubby until the summer of 1945. Following

VJ Day, RAF Strubby came under the RAF Flying College at RAF Manby, remaining in this role up to its closure in 1972. Since the closure of the base, the airfield has been home to Strubby Gliding Club (which changed its name to the Lincolnshire Gliding Club in the 1990s), Woodthorpe Aquatics and the Woodthorpe Kart Club, which occupies a large section of the field and buildings.

Legend has it that during the 1940s, a Lancaster Bomber returning to the base crashed close to the hangar and went up in a ball of flames, killing all on board. Although unsubstantiated, this story has been recounted several times and is believed to be the back story to a series of hauntings that have been experienced in and around the base over the years. The pilot of the stricken bomber is said to be the ghostly 'headless airman', who is reputed to have haunted the hangar and hard-standing area, at the Maltby end of the airfield, since the accident. It is in this location, in particular, that witnesses claim to have seen the terrifying apparition of a man dressed in the Second World War flying kit who, to their horror, has no head. During the time the base was operational, one RAF policeman was so disturbed by stories of the haunting that he refused to go anywhere near the hangar.

A factor that could have attributed to the policeman's reluctance to enter the hangar may have been a sighting of the apparition, which was recounted by one particular airman based at RAF Strubby. The airman claimed to have encountered the phantom during night-flying duties. The sighting disturbed the airman to such an extent that he had a mental breakdown and was hospitalised following his experience.

Can Anybody Hear Us?

Mystery surrounds a long-abandoned building that sits on the outskirts of Swinhope, just around the corner from Bishops Lane. The crumbling derelict facility is close to RAF Binbrook and is believed by some locals to have been a former listening station, which may have been a part of the ROTOR project during the Cold War. ROTOR was a huge and elaborate air-defence radar system, built by the British government in the early 1950s to counter possible attack by Soviet bombers. The system was built up primarily of war-era radar systems, and was used only briefly before being replaced by more modern systems.

A look at the building now reveals that it was surrounded by a double-layered brick wall, which, like the rest of the site, is overgrown and in a terrible state of disrepair. There are also 'man-made' holes in the floor outside, which may have been some kind of bunker system installed for emergencies, in case the building was destroyed by enemy planes.

During its days in service, it is said that the station was plagued by outbreaks of poltergeist activity and that this phenomena continued for several years. With so little known of its past, it is difficult to verify these claims. Perhaps the spirits, which are said to have haunted the building in the past, are still lingering within its deteriorating walls today.

The Spectres at the Station

Utterby Halt was on the line that ran between Louth and Grimsby and was opened on the 11 December 1905, by Great Northern Railway. Utterby was one of six halts opened by the Great Northern in 1905, prior to the introduction of a new railmotor service. It consisted of two short, low platforms, with a small wooden waiting room and a lamp on the 'up' platform and a lamp on the 'down' platform. The crossing-keeper's house was on the north side of a railway crossing, which was typical in design to others on the line. The line operated for just under fifty-six years, until it was closed on the 11 September 1961. All that remains of Utterby Halt now are the muddy tracks where the railway lines used to sit, the south-level crossing gate and a signal post on the south side of the crossing. The crossing-keeper's house still stands on the site, but it has been extended and is now in private occupation.

John Lancaster was employed by the railway as a length ganger, a job which involved walking lengths of train track checking bolts and keys, clearing any debris and cutting back vegetation along the line. One foggy January morning, John set off on his journey to Ludborough Station. As the fog had cut visibility to less than 10 yards, he decided to take the most effective route and walk along the railway track of the Louth to Grimsby line. John walked slowly and cautiously, listening for the sound of any approaching trains. A short distance into his walk, John heard the rattling sound of a particularly noisy freight train coming along behind him on the Louth line, which he was following. He stepped onto the adjacent track to let the train pass him by safely. Unfortunately, the noise of the freight train had drowned out the sound of the Cleethorpes to London train, which was masked by the dense fog and was now hurtling towards him.

The ghost of John Lancaster. (Illustration by Jason Day)

Unaware of the oncoming locomotive, John stood on the track, straight in its path, and was hit by the train. He was killed instantly, only half a mile from Ludborough Station.

Ever since the terrible accident, witnesses have reported seeing the form of John Lancaster walking the site of the former Halt. He has been seen most regularly in the area where the tracks used to lie (near to the level crossing), where he met his fate.

Although the station has been closed for many years, cars driving along Pear Tree Lane still have to cross the point where the track's level crossing used to be. At this point in the road, several motorists have reported their cars stalling for no reason at all, even motorists that have no previous knowledge of the site's tragic past. Witnesses are left even more baffled, as when they attempt to start their cars again, they immediately jump back into life and complete their journey without any hitches. One particular report of this phenomena occurring is particularly disconcerting and was, indeed, terrifying for the witnesses involved.

A couple were driving along Pear Tree Lane when they began experiencing mechanical trouble with their vehicle. Their car stammered to a halt just outside the former Utterby Halt crossing-keeper's house, at the point where the train tracks for the level crossing used to sit. The driver attempted to start the car, but it seemed that it would be to no avail, the car was to all intents and purposes, dead. Suddenly, the couple heard the unmistakeable sound of an approaching train. They sat in the car, frozen with fear, literally too terrified to move. As they sat frozen in the car, awaiting the impact, they reported actually feeling the train pass straight through themselves and their vehicle. The train passed over the former crossing, through the car and its occupants, and headed into the distance. All was quiet again and eventually the petrified couple were able to move. The driver turned the ignition and the car started without any problems. It was only after the couple reported the mysterious incident, in 1980, that they found out that the line they had, had their terrifying ordeal on had been closed for nearly twenty years.

Is the ghostly train of Utterby Halt linked to the spirit of John Lancaster? Is it the same locomotive that took John's life in 1953? Or is the identity of the ghostly train another mystery to add to the paranormal history of Utterby Halt?

The Spectral Clergyman

All Saints' Church is set in the centre of Waltham village, 4 miles south of Grimsby. A lively and committed congregation, the members are inclusive in their approach, welcoming people from many Christian traditions, whilst valuing their roots and worship in the Church of England.

In the winter of 2000, a local woman was attending a carol singing service at the church, looking forward to the Christmas festivities that were fast approaching. The church was very crowded and the woman sat with her party waiting for the choir to make their way down the central isle to their pews, which were situated towards the back of the building on the right hand side.

Whilst she waited, the woman looked over to the choir's pews and saw what appeared to be a man of the cloth dressed in what she described as 'old-fashioned robes'. The man was reading from a hymn book. As she continued to watch him, the woman realised that she could actually see the wall of the church through the man and that he was not the solid form she thought he was. The woman began to try and rationalise what she was seeing and looked around the immediate vicinity of the man, to see if there was any logical explanation for what she was observing. She spent five minutes looking around, trying to eliminate possible natural causes for the apparition and discovered there were no windows nearby or anything else that could be projecting the image, just solid stone walls.

She then heard the choir begin to make their way down the central isle and briefly turned her head for a few seconds to watch them. As she turned back to area where the apparition had been, she discovered that he had vanished.

She discussed her experience with other members of her group but none of her party had seen the phantom clergyman. The woman cannot find a rational explanation for what she saw at All Saints' Church, but she did say that what she witnessed did not scare her; instead it left her with a warm feeling of well being.

Bibliography

BOOKS

Brandon, D. & Brooke, A., *Shadows in The Steam* (The History Press, 2009)
Chambers, R. *The Book of Days* (W&R Chambers, 1869)
Halpenny, Barrymore B., *Ghost Stations 1* (L'Aquila Publishing, 2008)
Page, W., *A History of the County of Lincoln: Volume 2* (Victoria County History, 1906)

MAGAZINES

Nymh, T., 'An introduction to Ghostbusters UK', *The Witch Tower*, Vol. 4, Issue 1,
  Autumn Equinox/Samhaim 2007
Upchurch, P., 'Goodbye to an old friend', *Key Frame* magazine
'Lincolnshire bewitched Farm', *Skegness Magazine*

NEWSPAPER ARTICLES

Brookes, T., 'Shedding light on the Hubbard's Hillss ghost', The *Louth Leader*
  (20 August 2003)
Wood, L., 'Putting a light on the spirit world', *Grimsby Evening Telegraph* (June 2005)

'When polling day led to riots', *Grimsby Evening Telegraph* (28 May 2009)
'Spooky goings-on at town shop', *Grimsby Evening Telegraph* (9 April 2010)
'Two poltergeist cases', *Journal of the Society for Psychical Research* (12 October 1905)
'Village witchcraft', *Liverpool Echo* (25 January 1905)
'The Lincolnshire witch', *Liverpool Echo* (25 January 1905)
'Incredible stories of witchery at Binbrook', Louth *and North Lincolnshire News*
  (21 January 1905)
'Market Rasen', *Louth and North Lincolnshire News* (21 January 1905)
'Bewitched Binbrook farm', *Louth and North Lincolnshire News* (28 January 1905)

'Devil worshippers and their sick sacrifices', The *Louth Leader* (14 January 2004)
'Experts claim church is paranormal paradise', The *Louth Leader* (22 January 2004)
'Ghost hunters descend on village', The *Louth Leader* (26 October 2004)
'Satanists' turned away from church', The *Louth Leader* (3 November 2004)

TELEVISION

Elliott, J., 'Ghosts cast darker shade on store', BBC News (28 May 2005)
Living With The Dead, 'The Grimsby Scratcher', Living TV (2008)

WEBSITES

www.bbc.co.uk
www.british-history.ac.uk
www.disused-stations.org.uk
www.fightercontrol.co.uk
www.ghosts-uk.net
www.grub-ghosthunters.co.uk
www.hauntedlincolnshire.co.uk
www.hubbardshills.co.uk
www.jasonday.co.uk
www.localhistories.org/grimsby.html
www.nelincs.gov.uk/art-culture-and-leisure/museums-and-galleries/
    fishing-heritage-centre/
http://nightowlsparanormalinvestigations.webs.com
www.paranormaldatabase.com
www.peterunderwood.org.uk
www.phantomencounters.co.uk
www.philwhyman.com
www.rodcollins.com
www.spr.ac.uk
www.thefishy.co.uk
www.thisisgrimsby.co.uk
www.traciewayling.com
www.trueghoststories.co.uk
www.urbanghostsmedia.com
www.urbanlincs.co.uk
www.wikipedia.org
www.whitenoiseparanormalradio.co.uk
www.words.inpurespirit.com

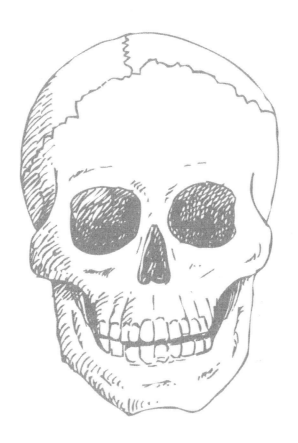

Other titles published by The History Press

Haunted Scunthorpe
JASON DAY

Haunted Scunthorpe guides you through the town's paranormal hotspots and
follows the apparitions into the surrounding villages and beyond. Including
previously unpublished haunting accounts from the author's own case files, this
collection of local hauntings has something for everyone. It is guaranteed to
entertain and spook anyone interested in Scunthorpe's ghostly history.

978 0 7524 5521 1

Paranormal Essex
JASON DAY

Join paranormal investigator Jason Day on a tour around one of England's oldest
and most paranormally active counties. Visit the site of the 'Most Haunted House
In England' at Borley, encounter the mysterious Spider of Stock, witness an RAF
pilot's shocking near miss with a UFO over the skies of Southend, and find out
how the infamous 'Witchfinder General' served as judge, jury and executioner in
Manningtree.

978 0 7524 5527 3

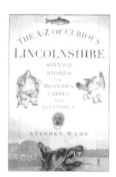

The A-Z of Curious Lincolnshire
STEPHEN WADE

This volume is filled with hilarious and surprising examples of folklore, eccentrics,
and historical and literary events, all taken from Lincolnshire's tumultuous history.
There has always been much more to Lincolnshire than farmland and seaside towns:
this is the county that brought us Lord Tennyson, John Wesley and, in contrast,
William Marwood, the notorious hangman; here too were found the Dam Busters
and the first tanks.

978 0 7524 6027 7

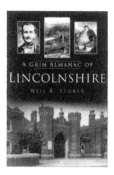

A Grim Almanac of Lincolnshire
NEIL R. STOREY

A Grim Almanac of Lincolnshire is a day-by-day catalogue of 365 ghastly tales from
around the county. Full of dreadful deeds, macabre deaths, strange occurrences
and heinous homicides, this almanac explores the darker side of Lincolnshire's
past. If you have ever wondered about what nasty goings-on occurred in the
Lincolnshire of yesteryear, then look no further – it's all here, and if you have the
stomach for it, then read on. . .if you dare!

978 0 7524 5768 0

Visit our website and discover thousands of other History Press books.
www.thehistorypress.co.uk